❧ THE INGENUE IN WHITE ❧

REFLECTIONS OF A COSTUME DESIGNER

". . . Marcia's great love of plays is the most wonderful gift she has to share . . . I've been a professional costumer for twenty-five years, and I walked away with a deeper appreciation of the work I do every day."

— Carolyn Keim, Costume Director, ACT Theatre

" 'Great design incorporates expectations and surprise,' observes author Marcia Dixcy Jory — and so does her book! . . . Intelligent, witty, and eloquent."

— Michael Bigelow Dixon, Literary Manager, Guthrie Theater

Published by
Smith and Kraus, Inc.
177 Lyme Road, Hanover, NH 03755
www.smithkraus.com

First edition: May 2004
9 8 7 6 5 4 3 2 1

Cover and text design by Freedom Hill Design, Reading, Vermont
Cover illustrations by Marcia Dixcy Jory

Library of Congress Cataloging-in-Publication Data

Jory, Marcia Dixcy.
The ingenue in white : reflections of a costume designer /
Marcia Dixcy Jory.
p. cm. -- (Art of theater series)
ISBN 1-57525-331-3
1. Costume design. I. Title. II. Series.
TT507 .J69 2003
792.02'6'092--dc22

2003044294

❧ The Ingenue in White ❧

REFLECTIONS OF A COSTUME DESIGNER

Marcia Dixcy Jory

Art of Theater Series

A SMITH AND KRAUS BOOK

SMITH AND KRAUS

the art of theater series

Accommodating the Lively Arts:
An Architect's View

The Front Page:
From Theater to Reality

A Cat's Diary:
How the Broadway Production of Cats was Born

Chekhov: Letters about the Theater

500 Years of Theater History from the Actor's Theatre of Louisville
Classics in Context Series

Let Me Set the Scene:
Twenty Years at the Heart of British Theatre 1956–1976

On Broadway, Men Still Wear Hats:
Fascinating Lives Led on the Borders of Broadway

A Shakespearean Actor Prepares

DEDICATION

For my father Thomas Dixcy

Contents

Chapter One

Angels on the Head of a Pin
MYSTERIES OF THEATRICAL DESIGN

Pat Zipprodt is dead. For many who read her obituary in *The New York Times*, she was a passing footnote, another interesting character having lived a rich, full life, unknown and extraneous to most. But for the majority of people working in theater and for all of us in costume design, her death left a large void. Though I didn't know her, she was an inspiration. Once, I heard her speak. She came to my graduate school to discuss her work and career as a theatrical designer. Her talk focused on fitting a large number of angels on the head of a pin. I remember her staring up with wide-eyed penetration at the imagined pin, which she held in her right hand, high in the air, conjuring the angels to leap for it with her left. She had wild, reddish hair and charismatic intensity, and I can still almost see the tiny angels hovering above her.

Pippin had recently opened on Broadway. Zipprodt, a three-time Tony Award–winner, had designed the showstopping costumes, and I wanted to hear detailed insider information. How had she come up with the idea of putting masks on the back of the dancers' heads? Where did she shop the fabrics and trims, how did she make the flexible armor? Instead, this business about angels and pins, and I wasn't quite sure what to make of her. Remembering the scene, I'm struck by how little we students could appreciate what she was trying to convey. We were eager to see her beautiful sketches. She threw them down rather dismissively, remarking only that her drawing ability had improved over time. Each of us craned to see Zipprodt's renderings up close. Like aspiring artists in a museum who push their way forward to see every brush stroke on a famous painting, we hoped that by taking in how she laid down pigment on the page, we might thereby absorb some of her genius.

Pat Zipprodt was trying to explain her genius, though she certainly would not have termed it that. She was metaphorically describing the intangible and evanescent unfolding, which for the sake of simplicity, I will call the creative process: the glory of it and the mystery and the tremendous choreographic complexity. She was speaking from the heart to a bunch of naïve pretenders about the inner workings of an art form we were scrambling to master. Just learning to handle the tools of our trade (fashion history, uniforms, formal wear, figure drawing, painting, properties of fabrics, patterning, cutting, sewing, millinery, mask making, to name the basics) seemed such an insurmountable task. We were far from ready to explore the soul of it all.

Over the years, I learned more about Pat Zipprodt. Increasingly, and unbeknownst to her, my determination to be a costume designer was guided by her example. I took it as a sign that, before learning her trade at the Fashion Institute of Technology, she had attended the same college as I, a liberal arts institution for women lacking what anyone could call a theater department. She graduated with a degree in sociology. One of the zaniest, most colorful, crafty, textural, sensual, and creative designers on Broadway was a liberal arts scholar! Until discovering Pat Zipprodt's educational background, I had grown mildly ashamed of my own beginnings, studying philosophy and literature.

When I went to graduate school, to get fine arts and technical training, I could barely sew, didn't know a gore from a grommet, and was almost laughed out of the costume shop for spending an entire evening inserting an Elizabethan sleeve into the neck hole of a bodice. Desperately trying to remedy my practical ignorance, I dove headlong into the crafts with which so many of my fellow classmates had been wrangling since the early days of their undergraduate BFA programs. Why in the world had I bothered with the aesthetic theories of Kant when I should have been learning to pattern a medieval kyrtle? As it turned out, I did need to pattern a medieval kyrtle, as I needed to learn the shapes and seams of countless other forgotten fashion landmarks. Acquiring those complex skills made me a more competent and assured designer. (My father archly showed off a bow tie I made him for Christmas one year, telling his friends and business acquaintances that it had only taken me seven years of higher education to accomplish it.) But beneath every ruche and furbelow that I stitched lurked an unseen passion: I loved plays. I loved reading them, listening to them, watching them. I loved discussing plays. My work as a costume designer, which now accounts for over half my life, has been fueled and sustained by that love. My research has been devoted to understanding plays better. My sketches described their characters, and my sewing served to make them more dazzling to the eye.

I don't count myself the equal of Pat Zipprodt, but I believe I have some appreciation for her attraction to a profession that exercises the mind and the hand in equal parts. Sociology is the study of human behavior and interactions, so to a great extent is dramatic literature. My interest in plays was bolstered by my interest in how people behave with one another. Why do they do the things they do and what are the consequences? Overlay sociology with metaphor and personal perspective — the result is drama. What makes costume design so interesting to me is that rather than responding to a work of dramatic literature as a purely intellectual, critical exercise, a theatrical designer joins her own creative sensibility and artistic skill with the poetic genius of the playwright. Costume design is premised on the ability to form a personal connection with an author's work. How have I been so lucky as to link my consciousness to Marivaux's? My job is really a kind of salaried time-travel. It requires the study of history, knowledge of the decorative arts, an examination of psychology. It's also like painting in motion. A costume designer works with composition, value, and color as does any artist. She analyzes character and monitors behavior as does any social scientist. She identifies theme, plot, and style as does any literary analyst. Not claiming expertise in any of these fields, a costume designer enjoys juggling. She likes to keep several balls in the air, thereby never tiring of the one in hand.

I don't know that costume design is a purely creative enterprise. It can be, but that's not its salient attribute. More like a game of concentration, costume design requires the kind of mind that likes to remember seemingly trivial visual symbols and combine them accurately. There may be nothing new under the sun. A theatrical designer doesn't care. She's supposed to be a thief. Her job isn't necessarily to come up with something that has never been seen. Rather, it is to find shapes and symbols that have appeared in a variety of times and places and to arrange them in a sympathetic universe. If she's lucky, she'll combine the right ingredients for a chemical reaction. That is, if a designer picks and chooses from her research, and makes the appropriate adaptations to synthesize with the choices of her other collaborators (the director, set designer, lighting designer, sound designer, choreographer, and actors), a theatrical transformation will take place that will merge words, sounds, images, and actions in a way that will communicate to the audience. Does this sound suspiciously like angels leaping onto the head of a pin?

Since the "stage picture" is a combination of actors, sets, costumes, and lights, extensive communication is required to orchestrate a balanced and effective whole. Talking would be the most obvious method of bringing about harmony, but among designers, talk is not always the most direct path to understanding. I once had a truly intriguing collaborative experience involving a set designer with whom talk was virtually impossible. I was designing the costumes in America for a production that had originated in Hungary. The play was directed by Laszlo Marton who runs Theatre Vig in Budapest. Laszlo's longtime design collaborator Miklos Feher accompanied him to adapt his original set to a stage whose dimensions were entirely different from those in Budapest. My costumes were to echo the spirit of the originals, though Laszlo and Miklos were open to new ideas and a wider range of materials than those available in Hungary, which at the time was under Soviet control. I was completely aware that Miklos was to be the overall artistic authority on anything concerning the design of this production. Since Miklos

was at least twenty years older than I and represented the highly sophisticated world of Eastern European theatrical design, which I
held in great respect, I was honored to defer to him. Laszlo spoke
perfect English, but Miklos did not speak one word.

Many times during the weeks of rehearsal and preparation,
Laszlo and Miklos made unexpected visits to the costume shop. Laszlo was the diplomat and translator, though his graceful European
manners seemed entirely incongruous in the low-ceilinged, clut-
tered washroom where I could usually be found working on masks
and dyeing fabrics. Miklos was a short, square man with a leonine
shock of white hair and a large mustache that made him resemble a
benign walrus. He moved slowly and silently, examining with care
whatever projects lay out in plain view. Sometimes Laszlo would ask
him a question in Hungarian, and Miklos would speak briefly in a
gravelly but sonorous voice, often smiling over at me as he did. Miklos' smile literally spread across his entire face, narrowing his eyes to
wrinkled slits. These smiles became increasingly dear to me, though
they occasionally accompanied a correction. When suggestions were
made, through Laszlo's translation, they were usually metaphorical or
thematic in nature. The impact of a mask, I might be told, should ultimately not detach the audience from a character but should encourage them to believe in his goodness or innocence.

During final dress rehearsals, Miklos occasionally approached
me in the darkened and deserted house as we awaited some lighting
change or technical cue. Sometimes he would say a word or two to
me, pointing to a character onstage, smiling and nodding his head
slightly to the side. Usually it was unnecessary for me to bother Laszlo for a translation. I could tell when Miklos liked something, and
when he didn't; the problem was fairly easy to identify, so much had
my eye and spirit become attuned to his.

Opening night after the play, there was a large party in a restaurant that adjoined the theater. I came upon Miklos, standing serenely at the bar. In a spirit of celebration, I offered congratulations, and not wanting to abandon him, continued to chat as if he could understand me. Miklos responded, and aided by our complimentary champagne, the conversation proceeded from that evening's performance to theater and design in general. I mixed in some high school French and he had, by that time, acquired a word or two of English. In the end, we gave up words and began drawing our ideas. I still have the cocktail napkin with an image Miklos used to describe our work.

This picture remains the number-one, best thing I ever learned in a bar. Additionally, it eloquently explains what I love about designing for the theater.

In its most mundane form, I think of my job as a matter of problem solving. I work within restrictions. The theater space, the play, the director, the set, the actors — numerous factors circumscribe my choices into smaller and smaller concentric spheres. Beginning with a theoretical debate over Hamlet's sanity, my design process will likely end with the more practical and specific question: Do his shoes fit? But in its Platonic ideal form, my job is exactly what Miklos drew. Every play gives me new opportunity to answer profound questions — so all that philosophy wasn't wasted! I'm not saying my answers are always correct or even complete, but that's one of the beauties of theater. The stage is like one of those dime-store children's drawing boards. After scribbling, you pull up the plastic sheet, all your markings are erased, and then you try again. The lack of permanence is freeing, and much of the fun is in starting over. Every time I conspire to fill an empty theater, I learn something or see something from a new perspective. I communicate with people unknown to me about the workings of the world, as we all struggle to decipher it.

Back when I was a student trying to make sense of those angels on the head of a pin, I figured Pat Zipprodt was talking about winged directors and actors and the like: the many people cooperating to make a production hold together as a unified conception. (It *is* just short of miraculous that so many disparate egos come together under intense time pressure to accomplish intangible goals of questionable necessity.) Or perhaps Zipprodt's angels on the pin were another version of Miklos' question mark. Theater gives its designers an opportunity to convene their dreams and discoveries. We may reinvent the past, explicate the present, or fantasize the future. Costume design, in all its frivolous detail, is a cog in the theatrical process, whose aim is understanding. The minutiae of my work combines in a theatrical attempt to extract meaning from the seemingly chaotic events of human existence.

Chapter Two

The Ingenue in White

MAKING THE IDEAL REAL

Before there is a design, there is a mental image. Whether this image proceeds from a lifetime of seeing and accumulating or emanates mysteriously from some unconscious creative spring is interesting to debate. The source of human imagination became a topic of particular significance to me after a head injury temporarily altered my memory and thereby my image-making ability. I was hit broadside in an automobile, and my unfortunate head bounced off a metal door frame and hit the iron stand of a dress dummy wedged between the front seats of my Fiat. ("Have mannequin, will travel" was the motto of my early years as a freelance costume designer.) During the following six months I experienced "retrograde amnesia," meaning my memory came and went at will, not my will but the will of the temporarily bollixed circuitry in my brain. Shocking to me who spent, and continues to spend, generous amounts of time staring out windows adrift in reverie, in losing my memory, I seemingly lost my ability to fantasize. From this experience, I became convinced that memory is the raw material of imagination. By losing access to my brain's stored images, I was unable to create new images.

To a costume designer, the loss of her ability to make mental images might be akin to an accountant losing the ability to add and subtract. A costume designer is an image-monger. From the words of a playwright, she imagines a picture of each character to which she gives form first as a two-dimensional sketch, and then as a three-dimensional arrangement of fabric and human shape. Barring amnesia, this would be a fairly simple process if she worked alone, culling images from her mental storehouse of information. But she is a collaborator, working with a number of equally imaginative people — the playwright, the director, the actor, the set and lighting designers, to name a few — who come to the table with their own backlog of stored memories and associations, predisposing them to various personal slants on the characters. Optimally, the costume designer is politic, resourceful, and inspired enough to gather shards of information from all of the above and come up with a transcendent image for each character, capturing everyone's quintessential points while appearing unique and exciting. She makes the ideal real.

Synthesizing the preconceptions of her collaborators with her own, a costumer is, more importantly, aiming to tap those of her audience. Preconceived notions may have their detractors, but they fuel the theater, where they are constantly being appealed to or debunked. Recognition of a character's personality or situation is arguably part of the experience of catharsis. Almost any high school has its Hamlet. Almost any business has its Willy Loman. Hedda Gabler may be one of a kind, but many women can identify with her dilemma. She was raised to be a bold and independent woman only to find herself confined in a marriage with a disappointing husband and a pregnancy that pointed to the end of art, romance, and adventure as she had always dreamed of them. In costuming *Hamlet*, *Death of a Salesman*, or *Hedda Gabler*, a designer works to facilitate the audience's identification of or with each character. What colors and fabrics a character wears, how ostentatious he appears, how he carries his clothes, how much he reveals his body are traits recognizable to many of us, no matter what the period. In the seventeenth century, Shakespeare places Hamlet in black, at odds with the opulent court that has prematurely shed its mourning for Hamlet's father. In Chekhov's nineteenth-century play *The Seagull*, the misfit Masha wears black because she claims to be in mourning for her life. Less than one hundred years later, in my high school in Verona, New Jersey, bad-boy Jonathan Marchand wore tight black denim jeans, a black shirt, and a black leather jacket. Despite his atrocious disciplinary record and his utter lack of respect for accepted secondary educational methods, Jonathan stunned our entire upwardly mobile community by being accepted to Yale Drama School. Types never die; they just reinvent themselves — and costume designers are there to note what makes them look like who they are.

There are types or even stereotypes that transcend the caprices of fashion and current events. Certain images stand the test of time, working their way into the collective unconscious and reappearing with indefatigable impact. These images earn the title of archetypes. The misanthrope in black, the harlot in red, or the ingenue in white require larger-than-life actors to embody them and confident, ingenious or historically savvy costume designers to clothe them. Given that they are highly idealized, these archetypical characters are particularly difficult to pin down. Because they live as images in the backs of so many minds, it's hard to come up with one look that satisfies everyone. It's like finding your dream house: Where is the perfect combination of rural and urban, sun-filled and cozy, spacious and affordable? The overriding challenge, in designing an archetypical character, is to satisfy the romantic expectations of the audience while maintaining the character's credibility as a human being.

Consider the ingenue in white. She inhabits a timeless, fictional plane, fitting chronologically between the real-life (and more event-oriented) confirmation girl and bride. She is largely an artistic construct, and as such, she comes color-coded. Beware the iconoclastic designer who tries to buck the system. I once changed Desdemona's fatal nightgown from white to silky red. Ostensibly, my reason was to make a very pale actress show up better on an all-white set. She did look remarkably shocking when laid out dead on the white sheets. (We'd all agreed that no stage blood was to be used: She was symbolically bloody.) But it just felt wrong. I know Desdemona is a married woman when we meet her, so not technically an ingenue; but no matter, she functions in *Othello* as the ingenue. She is the embodiment of youthful, female goodness, and as such, her heartfelt protestations of love and innocence were somehow debased in that red nightgown. She was less . . . pure. White carries tremendous iconographic clout. In Western culture, white clothing connotes cleanliness or rectitude of an almost unearthly sort. When did the last brown angel come to your door at Halloween? Though white knights and white-hatted sheriffs slash and shoot with the worst of them, their pristine image denotes moral superiority.

The vision of a young woman in white is out there in the image banks of almost anyone in Western society who has been exposed to even a modicum of art, literature (here I include fairy tales), or religious iconography. Sometimes playwrights specify that their young female characters appear in white, but in my experience, the director more often has that idea. Whether a fan of Wilke Collins, James Abbot McNeill Whistler, or innumerable other artistic forbears, a director is bound to demand a woman in white at some point in his theatrical career. The sex of this director may make a marked difference in his or her attitude about what the white garment is supposed to say or do.

Generally, male directors look on the ingenue in white as a tabula rasa. This attitude about girls in white dresses (with or without blue satin sashes) may be analogous to my preference for white walls in my workroom. If I have any one color on the wall, the room has too much specific impact. White allows me to project imaginary color, texture, and pattern on my surroundings, making them mentally transformable, open to any possibility. A tabula rasa ingenue is similarly open to transformation. Like Nina, also from Chekhov's *The Seagull*, an ingenue is often there to be plucked by various male characters, young and old. In more heroic terms, she exists to be rescued, discovered, or awakened. The key ingredient in this attitude, and the one that makes life difficult for the costume designer, is that the ingenue must be innocent — read nonsexual. The innocent ingenue may not dress to entice. Her nubile body must be hidden from view. By the time the costume designer outfits the ingenue in a suitably amorphous garment, the poor actress is liable to end up onstage looking vaguely dumpy, and the design perpetrator is stuck answering that most hated of questions, "How come she looked so much better in rehearsal?" The answer is, in rehearsal she was wearing a flimsy tank top and skintight biking shorts. She could move better and every-one enjoyed watching her! You can't cover her and see her at the same time.

Alternately, the hypothetical female director (or male director with a highly evolved anima) is out to fight against type. Her ingenue is usually trapped inside the white dress. The character's body is important in that it is severely corseted, boned, bustled, hoop-skirted, or strangled by a high collar. Here the difficulty for the costume designer is in coercing a very modern, probably athletic body into supremely uncomfortable and necessarily confining shapes. The actress must use her hateful undergarments from day one of rehearsal to block and form a physical performance within the parameters of considerable breathing, bending, and striding restrictions. How often have I been assured by an actress gazing into the fitting-room mirror that she loves her corset, only to hear later from the stage manager that she has never tolerated it for more than thirty minutes of a physically demanding rehearsal? By the time our twelve-hour dress rehearsal rolls around, the beleaguered actress is assuring everyone that she has experienced the sense memory of her corset and now wishes to act without it. Unfortunately, her costume will not fit her normal, uncorseted shape, and the ensuing pandemonium isn't fun. By the time the ingenue gets a white dress she can bear, she looks perfectly comfortable but hardly trapped. Another concept left on the drawing board.

Perhaps the reason so many "conceptual" costumes are more suited to drawing boards than to actors is that in trying to satisfy their thematic and artistic duties, they overstep their function as clothing. Clothes may undeniably rank as exquisite, abstract pieces of sculpture; they are unique moving collages of color and texture. But theatrical costumes are inextricably dependent on the actors who wear them. With all jealous respect for Bob Mackie's designs, only performers on the magnitude of Cher, Carol Burnett, or Barbie can really pull them off. Actors love to be enhanced by their costumes, but very few of my acquaintance like to be overshadowed by them.

Given the vast pool of young female actors fitted to play an ingenue, the one gifted and tenacious enough to be chosen for a main role in any professional production is seldom innocent or uninformed. If she is to be a tabula rasa ingenue, she's undoubtedly struggling to give a fulsome performance from the projected position of a nonperson. Alternately, if she's an ingenue fighting against type, she probably expects to breathe, move her arms, and bend at the waist. I have never seen an actress react with unfeigned pleasure when told that her costume's main point is to obscure or confine her. She is likely to cast her archetypal white dress, or by association its creator the costume designer, as her mortal enemy.

I still cringe at the memory of designing a production of *School for Wives,* which centers on the cloistering of a young girl by a jealous and tyrannical older guardian/suitor. The director, an Eastern European, conceived the play as an allegory for totalitarianism. Arnolf was the Soviet State; he wore black. Agnes, the sequestered woman/ child, represented a small nation traversed by the Danube; she wore white. The director was, in fact, an inspiring artist, and our comprehensive discussions of every character bore fruit in costume designs that excited us both, with one notable exception. Agnes eluded me. Sadly, this depersonalizing characterization eluded the actress playing Agnes, as well. Discussions and negotiations throughout our fittings were punctuated by her resigned but ironic eye-rolling. The director was dissatisfied by my attempts to make the actress feel somewhat attractive in her costume at the expense of making her look sufficiently demure. After rejecting two of my creations, one lovingly hand-smocked, the director insisted Agnes wear her rehearsal garment — a formless, battered white muumuu, pulled by the stage manager from a box of ragtag rehearsal costumes and much-hated by the actress and myself. Its appeal, from what I could discern, was that it had grown familiar to the director, made Agnes seem completely uninterested in her looks, and allowed her to move freely. These could be said to be positive points but for my belief that a costume fails completely when an actress feels unhappy in it. Her performance, however imperceptibly, is affected.

From this experience, I emerged a bit wiser to design more successful ingenues in various shades of white. Invariably the best results come by working from the inside out. Like her colleagues the actor and the director, a costume designer must read and reread a script, carefully interpreting each character's given circumstances, motivations, and reactions. Along with fine-toothed text analysis, costuming from the inside out involves a combination of empathy, projection, people-watching, and psychology. A character may represent an idea or an ideal, but what he or she is wearing has to represent a practical series of choices and necessities as well. Shakespeare's Perdita, Wilder's Emily, Chekhov's Irina, Williams's Laura, and Strindberg's Miss Julie are among many white-dress candidates. Surely they share little in common except sex and age. Much depends on their relationships with their parents. Who chose the dress? Who made it? What materials could she afford or find? Is there a special occasion? Is she trying to appear older, being forced to appear younger? Has she been exposed to society? Is she physically active? What does the character feel about herself? What attitude does she have about her body? How much is she aware of her body's impact on others? Certain basic questions must be asked whether you're choosing the clothes for Lizzy Borden or Pollyanna.

Working on a production of *The Tempest*, a director might very well ask that Miranda look as though she just stepped out of a fresco by Sandro Botticelli. It then becomes the costume designer's job to turn a two-dimensional, pastoral ideal into a functional piece of clothing on a living human being. Perhaps the dress is sea-stained and tattered around the hemline. Perhaps Miranda pulls the back of her skirt through her legs and hitches it up to the front of her vine-covered waistband so that she can run about the island. Alternately, she could look elaborately robed and immaculately appointed and all could be attributed to Prospero's magic staff. But little would be revealed about Miranda. In truth, she has very few lines, and if she appears as an impenetrable paragon of Renaissance beauty, how much humanity and tenderness is lost from the production?

Trying to get inside any character, I have been most successful taking my cue from the actor. Yes, this has to do with how the actor looks: fair or dark, statuesque or sylphid. Quite often, the person cast looks nothing like the character I have imagined. This is a good thing; if the director is casting purely based on looks, we're all in trouble. Though it sounds like the oldest cant, what's important, even when it comes to style, is only partly external. Short or tall, there are an infinite number of intellectual, emotional, and behavioral nuances that any two actresses could bring to the roles of Hermia and Helena in Shakespeare's *A Midsummer Night's Dream*. How she walks, how she laughs or cries, how she listens — when an actor embodies a role, the character is humanized in an absolutely specific way. The key is to identify what quality makes an actor light up her role. Once that becomes clear, questions concerning her clothing are far more interesting to answer.

In a production of *Romeo and Juliet*, I knew that my Juliet was a wildly physical actress, daringly emotional and expressive. She had a compact, dancer's body, black hair, and a deep, warm complexion. Her hair was cut short, just below her ears. Determining that an elaborate wig and long ornate gown would detract from her freedom and spontaneity, I advocated moving the period of the production at least to the twentieth century. The set designer agreed that the performers should look like people recognizable to a contemporary audience rather than appear as romantic figures from Italian art history. The setting, we agreed, could far predate the costumes, as one sees photographs of contemporary Italians walking among architectural remnants of the Quatrocento and before. We finally set the production in late 1920s Italy, as Fascism was beginning to split the country. The Montagues represented the aristocratic, anti-Fascist intellectuals, and the Capulets became members of the wealthy middle class who stood behind many Fascist innovations. I actually planned my designs around Juliet, and she did wear white, in various tones and textures, throughout the play. Since the set, based on a magnificently painted Renaissance courtyard still in existence, was richly colored, costumes other than Juliet's were carefully dyed or chosen to harmonize in values lighter or darker than those of the surround. Juliet's dresses were the most simple in both color and style. The straight lines of the 1920s, so difficult for more curvaceous actresses to wear, were perfect for our actress. Seamed with extra gussets and godets, her clothing allowed her to move effortlessly. The wonderful lines of her body were evident through the thin silks and linens, though the cut of her garments was youthful and not ostensibly alluring. Would the same approach have been successful had Juliet been pale and ethereal? I doubt it.

My solution to the ingenue in white, or any theatrical stereotype for that matter, is to humanize her as quickly as possible. A costumer must be able to recognize and empathize with each character. It's not enough that the designer walk a mile in the ingenue's shoes; she's got to pick the shoes to walk in. Inquiries must be made. What is the character's arc in this production? What are her circumstances when we first meet her; how do we last see her? In what way is her situation familiar and in what way unique. Who is the actress? How can her strengths be enhanced? How can her weaknesses be diminished? By the time many of these questions are answered, countless possibilities have been eliminated and numerous human connections have been established. Additionally, such concrete questions may actually have answers that can be agreed upon. How can she look beautiful? How can she look innocent? How can she look unrealized? These questions are open to endless speculation. It's very hard to draw a sketch of open-ended possibility, and it's even harder to buy it or sew it.

As the ingenue in white makes her journey from the mind to the stage, she achieves tangible, identifiable form through the accumulation of specific thoughts, emotions, actions, and physical details. She must function as the embodiment of a widely acknowledged preconceived image, and as such must be immediately familiar to the audience. Additionally, she represents an intangible ideal, a creative paradigm, and so should appear more significant or unusual than a person who might be seen any day on the street. Costuming the ingenue in white, then, is an arrangement of the familiar in pursuit of the unique. A costume designer uses her faculties to call up familiar details of people and place. She imaginatively reworks specific choices to create an image that she hopes will be both acceptable and, in some greater way, provocative to an audience. Audience members, one hopes, pick up clues from that which is familiar in the images before them and, by imaginatively linking these specifics to kindred information in their own memories, come up with fresh and illuminating insights. With the cooperation of actress, director, designer, and audience, the ingenue in white, or any stage image, will transcend the sum of her parts and will enjoy ongoing life in the minds of her beholders.

Chapter Three

The Wolf in Sheep's Clothing

WHAT'S THE CHARACTER TRYING TO SHOW AND WHAT'S HE TRYING TO HIDE?

Beneath every human façade exists a character who may or may not be truthfully represented by his look. The ingenue in white is not the only one who gets trapped within an image. It happens all the time, in real life as well as theater.

Remember the high school prom? For most Americans it's a standard rite of passage, and ceremonial costumes figure importantly into the proceedings. My direct experience is with the female half of this event. One of its crucial components involves *the hairdo*. At least in my day, you went to the hair salon and paid good money for some elaborately lacquered upsweep. Then you came home, burst into tears, fought with your mother, and combed it out at the last minute, just before your date arrived at the door with a corsage, which probably looked really stupid with your dress, even if it was a wristlet. Female or male, most prom-night celebrants have gone through the process of constructing an external image premised on accepted custom and, with more difficulty, tried to maintain some sense of individuality or internal comfort while shrouded in their unfamiliar façade. In less extreme fashion, people walk the streets daily in various forms of disguise. Part of the fun of costuming is identifying how much a character is revealed or concealed by what he wears and how much he is "at home in his skin."

As the brilliant art and costume historian Anne Hollander has pointed out, "Clothes make, not the man but the image of the man . . . " Since the first fig leaf, clothing has evolved from its pragmatic origins, which were undoubtedly to cover and protect genitalia, keep people warm and dry, and carry things. Somewhere along the way, an early human got the idea that body coverings could embellish and distinguish people. Along with its protective and decorative functions, clothing has historically been used to identify people: to show rank, profession, or affiliation. Though any Roman citizen could wear the *toga pura*, a symbol of manhood, only a senator, magistrate, or noble was allowed the honor of decorating his toga with a straight band of Tyrian purple. A triumphant general, a governor, or an imperial figure might wrap himself in the exclusive silk *toga picta* elaborately embroidered in gold. Today, male political figures have traded in their togas for well-tailored navy-blue wool suits, white shirts, and red ties. Though they don't have exclusive rights to this outfit, they stick to it with little variation, guided by unwritten strictures that seem to rule with less ambiguity than can be found in constitutional law. Uniforms, both official and unofficial, are an integral part of human civilization.

Within most societies, official uniforms function in a number of capacities. As has been mentioned, a particular uniform may identify a person's profession. Doctors, policemen, and firemen wear uniforms that are functionally adapted to the activities of their jobs. Additionally, their specialized clothing augments their public legitimacy, setting them apart as individuals qualified to perform these jobs. In uniform, a policeman or a fireman may make unpleasant intrusions into people's lives that might otherwise be unacceptable. Don't ask me why, but I'm uncomfortable when a doctor doesn't wear a white coat. The white coat represents her skill and scientific knowledge; it also plays down her individual humanity or personality. An official uniform tends to neutralize an individual in a way that allows him to cross personal, no-trespass zones. As the ultimate extension of this phenomenon, a soldier, anonymously protected and glorified by his uniform, may kill — a transgression of the most fundamental human law. Uniforms are accepted signs that the wearer has been accorded particular powers that plainclothesmen may neither want nor merit.

Unofficial uniforms, like that of the politician, function slightly differently than those of a policeman or soldier. They evolve as a matter of custom and are worn as a matter of personal choice, either conscious or unconscious. By adolescence, humans have already begun to segregate themselves by image — or unofficial uniform. In the twenty-first century, goths and skaters have replaced hoods and greasers, while more tradition-bound preppies have endured, almost unchanged, for fifty years or more. Public school authorities have tried to squelch the factionalizing tendency of such unofficial uniforms by instituting official ones. These usually consist of khaki pants or skirts, belts, and blue or white, collared shirts — which is basically a preppy look, and so unfairly judgmental as to what is the "right" kind of image. (We know what group the school administrators belonged to in high school.) Many such dress codes are eventually abandoned as teachers find themselves spending inordinate amounts of time squelching individual violations of the institutionalized uniform. For young adults, image is tremendously important. Maybe it has to do with mating rituals, allowing birds of a feather to identify one another.

In the adult workplace, unofficial uniforms prevail as surely as they do in high school. Businessmen and women adhere variously to unstated dress codes according to their professions. Obviously, a different image will prevail in an advertising agency where "creativity" is the marketable commodity, than would be acceptable in a bank where order and reliability are what the customer looks for. I was told by a fellow mother that the principal of my daughter's future middle school was basically "a suit." When I asked her to explain what that was supposed to mean, she said that he was good at fund-raising and dealing with county administrators but had little time for the students or parents. Suits, like white collars, are the unofficial uniforms of money and power. Their wearers are not considered to be "people persons." The mother who gave me the lowdown on this principal, though she worked at home as a highly paid technical writer, was dressed as a "soccer mom," whose unofficial uniform varies slightly according to region but basically consists of kid-friendly comfort clothes: jeans, brand-name sneakers, colorful knit tops, a sensible, perhaps expensive watch, earrings, and appropriate, high-end, techno-fiber outerwear.

Unofficial uniforms, like official ones, basically adhere to the functional demands of a person's daily life and work. This is truer of men's than women's clothing. Historically, men's clothes, while equally foible-ridden, ostentatious, or absurd, have been more adapted to comfort and movement than have women's. Even today, women holding powerful positions in business and government are somehow expected to pull off back-breaking hours and harried activity in high heels! Male movers and shakers may take the time to comb over their bald spots and tie their ties, but few would wax their eyebrows or put up with a day in control-top pantyhose. Functionality in unofficial clothing remains sex-linked. In terms of living the feminist ideal, women in the police force and the army have it all over Hillary Clinton and Gloria Steinem. So, form may trump function in the dialectical creation of unofficial uniforms.

Costume designers fascinate themselves with the study of unofficial uniforms. Any bus stop, any visit to the lawyer's office, any cross-country road trip may be a college course in the sociology of costume. Like his compatriot, the birder, the costumer is a demon for taxonomy. Slight variations of belt buckling and cuff turning are noted with the diligence a birder might apply to the observation of feather and beak length. In addition to observation, a costumer adds a layer of supposition to her studies. What do people choose to wear to align themselves with a group? And within the parameters of an unofficial costume, what are the nuances that individualize them? Like the high school prom date, how a person feels (or identifies himself) inside his uniform may be at odds with what he is trying to project as an image. Contradictions between what a person says about himself by the outward appearance he contrives and what he feels or thinks about himself within the privacy of his unseeable self-image comprise the subtext of costume design.

The observation component of a costumer's taxonomy of clothes wearing, then, consists first of gathering information about the unofficial uniform of a group or segment of the population and, second, cataloguing slight variations within the uniform that might serve as indicators to the wearer's interior motivation or individual-

ity. Is a person positioning herself within or outside an easily identifiable "norm"? What is she trying to show, and what is she trying
to hide? Not everyone goes to elaborate lengths to identify or con-
ceal themselves through dress, but all people wear clothes, which
even by default display a good deal of information about them. The
master birder David Sibley can give you thirteen categories for identifying the feathers on the head of a song sparrow. I'll list a costumer's basic six for observing human plumage.

Wealth

Clothes cost money and everyone knows it. Throughout the centuries, clothing has helped to set the haves apart from the have-nots.
Servants have always worn different clothes from their masters, not
only because they could afford different materials — wool and hemp
on the former, silk and gold on the latter. The wealthy can pay others to do their work, and they wear clothes that reflect their leisured
state. No self-respecting courtier to Louis XIV could do much clean-
ing, cooking, or even writing with twelve inches of white lace cas-
cading from the sleeves of his doublet. No problem, all he had to do
was eat, stroll, and dance (he had gutsier clothes for hunting). He did-
n't have to worry much about dirtying fabrics that cost a life-time of
someone else's embroidering and tatting to produce. A lady of
Madame de Pompadour's circle, wearing a rigidly structured pannier
beneath her expansive skirt, extended her breadth about three feet on
either side. She could hardly walk into a room or perch upon a seat
without an entourage of less ungainly helpers to open her doors and
monitor her train, escorting her to her destination as tugboats bring
an ocean liner safely to harbor. For centuries, those who could afford

the finest footwear have deformed their feet, and I'm not just talking about the Chinese ladies who bound them. Within my lifetime, really elegant shoes were made to appear symmetrical, pinching the toes to a narrow point in the middle. Walking in such style was necessarily mincing, and over any extended period of time disabling, but who needs to walk if she can afford to ride or sit? Not satisfied with deforming their feet, wealthy women have spent at least five hundred years configuring their torsos into a multitude of shapes. Corsets, ruthlessly structured with hundreds of whalebone or metal stays, left little room for a lady's diaphragm to expand. Breathing and, consequently, active movement were severely restricted. Breathing, one assumes, was of secondary importance to a woman so fortunately untroubled by the exigencies of labor that she could devote her time to becoming an art object. The wealthy have always found ways to stylize and embellish their inactivity, while less wealthy people have had to accommodate, proportionate to their means of farming out labor, the necessity of moving and getting dirty.

Contemporary clothing continues to be a fairly reliable indicator of wealth. Manolo Blahnik shoes, costing upwards of several thousand dollars, would undoubtedly be unwearable for someone standing long hours on the hospital night shift. Fur coats are warm, but is that their major function? Accessories provide quick financial information to a clothes-watcher. They announce disposable income or credit rating with as loud a voice as the accessorizer wishes to employ. Handbags, briefcases, shoes, sunglasses, and, of course, watches can take a bite or a greedy gobble out of a pocket, and those who are willing to pay four figures and up for these items are buying them as much for the status they confer as for their craftsmanship and durability. Wealthy people often have multiples of the most expensive accessories, and either because they have acquired the habit of acquisition or because they need to remind people of their ability to make and spend money, they tend to update their collections long before their shoes are worn out or their watches stops running.

Even as wealth trickles down in our society, excess or scarcity is evidenced by how people dress and adorn themselves. As the flush years of the late twentieth century gave way to leaner times, many hairstylists reported a marked cutback in services. Where once there were a glut of customers willing to drop eighty dollars or more a month on hair coloring, an upturn of reformed brunettes followed, cutting their budgets and growing out their frosted streaks. Upkeep costs money, no matter who you are. Better technology and low-cost imitations have put some luxury items within the grasp of those who wish to assume the trappings of wealth. Acrylic nails give supermarket checkout girls hands that were once the sole domain of ladies who lunched. But take another look at the Band-Aids and callouses, also check out the rings; it's hard to fake Tiffany diamonds. Many people aspire to wear costly (or costly looking) clothing and accessories. They may actually like them, but they may also like to show they can afford them. You don't have to be a costumer to read a designer logo. Whether it's Chanel or Fubu, it's out there for everyone to see just as surely as the price tag on Minnie Pearl's hat.

Class

Closely allied to clothing's function as an indicator of income is its ability to separate class. Today it is perhaps more acceptable to talk about education or even race than class, but if one is producing plays from other periods and societies, class is often a factor that divides and distinguishes characters. Class differences have always been the stuff of drama. The seventeenth-century comedies of Moliere, the eighteenth-century works of Sheridan, the nineteenth-century plays of Ostrovsky and Chekhov, or the twentieth-century dramas of Tennessee Williams contain titanic mismatches of class and taste.

Though the nature and impact of class distinctions may be different in modern-day America from what existed in Louis XIV's France, the impact of class history, one could argue, still exists. In pre-industrial Western society, power, wealth, and high social rank (or class) went pretty much hand in hand. Lack of rank meant lack of clout, both of which meant lack of access to such privileges as property and sumptuous attire. Movement from the lower to the higher order of being was inflexible, infrequent, and accompanied only by preternatural talent, luck, or beauty. With the industrial revolution and the advent of the bourgeoisie, many people of modest backgrounds earned enough money to buy garments once affordable only to those with inherited wealth. How, then, does the aristocracy distinguish itself sartorially from the upstarts? Classically, the issue is said to be one of *taste*. Those who are born and bred to *good taste* acquire it from elegant grandparents, from their cronies at prep school, from those same sources who endow them with good manners and correct speech. Understatement is the hallmark of aristocratic good taste just as ostentatious display stereotypically marks the nouveau riche.

Today, some may still distinguish between those who show off their new money and those old money folks who have been born to privilege and demonstrate a more refined discretion in their expenditures. But with the advent of Hollywood's aristocracy and the proliferation of magazines and television programs profiling the rich and famous, new standards of what might be termed "high-class" taste are mingling with the old. The ministrations of Ralph Lauren and Martha Stewart have put good taste within reach of anyone with a credit card, and one is hard pressed to differentiate between the clothing choices of the purportedly upper-class characters in an A. R. Gurney play and the middle-class professionals in one by Donald Margulis. The trappings of wealth and privilege have indeed been scalped from America's dusty upper echelons and marketed to such a degree that class delineations in contemporary plays must be carefully handled by the costume designer lest they appear dated and derivative of Madison Avenue stereotypes.

Geography

Geographical location is to some degree discernable through clothing. The cliché that all New Yorkers dress head to toe in black has a reasonable basis in utility. First of all, everything black goes together and quickly. Fashionistas, whose American capital is New York City, have always touted the basic black dress, and in a city where people are habituated to walking and public transit, moving from office to nightclub with no home stop in between, black will go the distance. It matches the grime. You sit in some objectionable substance on the subway; not to worry, it won't show. You lean on a greasy counter, you step into who-knows-what on the street — same difference. Black tells no stories. Welcome to the city. You are costumed as one of a classically chic, urban-survivalist coterie.

In inverse fashion, people really do wear lighter colors in the south. Who knows why? Southerners may dress to deflect the blinding sunshine as it ricochets off the belvedere, or their sensibilities just may be more soft-hued and genteel. For whatever reason, you will see corporate executives in Louisville sporting pale blue summer suits. White shoes are prevalent on or off the golf course.

Climate, of course, has much to do with these variations. If you are costuming *Ice Fishing* by the Minnesota playwright Kevin Kling, it's going to require more wool than a production of *Picnic* by William Inge. Additionally, certain types of people are undoubtedly attracted to certain climates.

For whatever reasons, regional differences abound. Grunginess that might be considered chic in Seattle would not play in Atlanta. Visiting Santa Fe, I inevitably pick up an artsily hip garment or piece of jewelry that, as a middle-aged woman, I feel immediately ridiculous wearing when I'm outside the realm of the eternally suntanned, neo–Georgia O'Keefe new agers. Inside many women beats the heart of Annie Oakley, but a cowgirl outfit can slide by in only a few areas of the country — I don't care what Ralph Lauren says!

Age

Though age is purportedly a state of mind, it has a way of inflicting itself on the body. How much a person can do affects what he can wear. Granted, fifty-year-olds vary widely in being fit and young at heart, just as eighteen-year-olds are not always paragons of health and well-being. The boundary lines of age-appropriate dress do overlap. Women no longer assume the title of matron upon marriage nor do dowagers don black dresses and white bonnets. But despite modern advances in medicine, exercise equipment, and cosmetic surgery, some external differences still remain between the young and the old.

I don't care how much botox, collagen, and cellulite removal you use, the glory of youthful flesh just doesn't extend indefinitely after youth's first bloom. Seldom do you see (or seldom do you delight in seeing) a middle-aged woman wearing a transparent blouse with no foundation garment. Artificially structured and uplifted cleavage? Yes. But natural, gravity-defying curvaceousness? No. Correspondingly, most men past their youth seldom strip to the waist or wear Marlon Brandoesque T-shirts with impunity. You do see it, but when you do, the sporty fellow hardly looks younger than his years, just more foolish. Generally, unless they are gym rats, older men and women are not fond of their bare arms. (Gym rats, being the exception, insist on going sleeveless winter, spring, summer, and fall, no matter what their age.) Also, older legs, even the best of them, generally demand to be covered. For a woman, this may mean darker or opaque hose, even if she remains true to her mini.

Shoes become more sensible with the growing years. Feet have to bear a lot, and they become less adaptable to fashion as time goes by. As a costumer, I have found that there is no item of apparel about which people become more passionate than shoes. This passion has to do with comfort and security, which is perhaps slightly more important to the postfifty crowd, but also with style and custom. It stands to reason that with age, sense would overshadow style, but not invariably. I know a sixtyish French seamstress whose Achilles tendons have become so accustomed to her stiletto heels that she literally can't stand to walk barefoot. At home, she wears steeply arched espadrilles for comfort even to perform such perilous chores as fixing her roof! Obviously, not every sixty-year-old repairs her own roof, so energy and health have as much to do with how a person behaves and dresses as does age.

Health

People of any age in reasonable health can deal with a higher level of discomfort than can those who are infirm. In most decades, being fashionable or even well dressed has been synonymous with being uncomfortable. Starched shirts, tight vests, and sleek leather shoes conflict with physical happiness more than do unbuttoned polo shirts and slouchy sweaters. When one is trying to minimize physical aches and pains, why add to the problem by wearing clothes that are uncomfortable? Women, who have suffered since puberty under the edict that "it hurts to be beautiful," often abandon tight waistbands and cold legs when bad digestion and arthritis begin to take their toll. The big question is how much energy do we have to spare? When illness or disability is present, the energy-consuming physical demands of high fashion and exquisite grooming move low on the priority list.

There are countless subsets to these five categories: politics, religion, mental state — to name a few. Most of the finer divisions involve internal motivation versus external circumstance. Crossing into the area of motivation, the costumer, like the birder, relies on variations of behavior to augment information provided by outward appearance alone. Combining data about how a person acts with what a person looks like, a designer then calls upon her experience and psychological insight to form suppositions about the relationship of that person's emotions and intellect with his outward appearance. This internal/external dynamic can more simply be called a person's self-image.

Self-Image

This might well be the category that trumps all others when it comes to how a person presents himself to the world. Self-image may transcend the deprivations of age and ill-health. I've seen octogenarians, bent with age, clinging to walkers as they make the arduous trip to the dining room of their retirement community, dressed and groomed so impeccably that, insofar as style is concerned, they put their accompanying middle-aged children to shame. Self-image may drive the poor to appear rich (Eliza Doolittle) or the rich to appear poor (Ebenezer Scrooge). Self-image may make sexual predators of the homely (the Duchess of Windsor), fashion icons of the physically nondescript (Coco Chanel or Diana Vreeland), or pragmatic individualists of the lovely (Jane Goodall).

Self-image often works in counterpoint with practical necessity. Many a forty-something-year-old will wear tight blue jeans long after such attire has ceased to be comfortable or financially necessary. A shy and uncertain nineteen-year-old might hide behind a façade of paramilitary clothing, dyed black hair, and treacherous body piercings. Linked to this question of how one perceives oneself is the question of how one wants to be perceived by others and what sort of dichotomy exists between the two.

Some people live happily in the bunker provided by an appearance put together to protect their private natures from public scrutiny. Others have a more discordant relationship between what they feel like and what they look like. Either way, when a person looks in the mirror, does she see the same image that others see when they look at her? How accurate is anyone in accessing the impact of her appearance? Does the wolf think he looks good in sheep's clothing, and what do the sheep think?

Dramatic literature mines the wealth of tensions existing in the gaps between how people perceive themselves and how other people perceive them. In Tennessee Williams's *A Streetcar Named Desire,* Blanche DuBois is past her prime, penniless, homeless, and alcoholic. Even so, the image she maintains of herself as an aristocrat would never allow her to hock her finest clothing, ignore her grooming, or walk around the Kowalski apartment in an old bathrobe and slippers. In costuming Blanche, a designer must take into account that her given circumstances and self-image are at odds. She is still charismatic and sophisticated enough to dazzle Mitch and intimidate Stella, yet Stanley sees the desperation and shabbiness beneath her behavior. The inappropriate quality of Blanche's elegance must co-exist with her sensitive taste. Contradictions are arguably the most intriguing part of anyone's character. Recognizing the clothes-related signposts of those contradictions and using them to individualize a theatrical character is one of the most fascinating parts of a costume designer's job.

Using and applying observations about dress and image to costume any production is ultimately a subjective process. Given circumstances — such as the age, wealth, class, and probably even the geography of the characters — are likely to be similar in anyone's production of *Uncle Vanya.* But questions of personal image may vary wildly from production to production. I have designed *Vanya* twice and nothing differed so much in the two productions as the portrayal of Sonja.

My first *Vanya* was directed by a young American. Sonja was the absolute heart of this production. A lovely, robust blond was cast in the role in contrast to a gaunt, angular, dark Eleyna. Appropriately,

Sonja's clothes were simple and more suited to practical activity than were those of the more urbane and indolent Eleyna, but inappropriately, we conspired to make Sonja as attractive as possible, ignoring the many statements in the play that she was anything but. Being young ourselves, siding with Sonja, and wanting an attractive heroine, we gave in to what I consider the mistaken, though popular, practice of insisting that inner beauty be projected by outer.

My second production of *Vanya* was much less kind to poor Sonja. The Romanian auteur-style director saw Sonja as a comic character. Perhaps Sonja's insistence on the value of mortal toil and self-sacrifice for the collective good was too close to the director's deep-felt hatred of Communism. I'll never forget the absurd little hat he demanded for Sonja's first entrance; it was a straw confection that made her look like a yokel from Dogpatch U.S.A. I may not properly understand the comedic nature of Chekhov, or a Romanian under Soviet domination may have more dispassionately appreciated the ineffectual pretensions of pre-revolutionary Russians. In either case, I felt that all hope of conveying Sonja's inherently sincere and credulous character was overshadowed by the director's wish to make her appear as an absurdly stolid provincial.

Deciding just how much of a character's outer circumstances, inner workings, and social image can or should be projected by her clothing is a matter of designer/director discretion and dramatic genre. In the best of all worlds, a costume designer discusses a character's background and motivations with a director before ever putting pencil to paper. Too often, however, all discussion of the text and the subtext are subsumed by a director's drive to conceptualize and a designer's compulsion to decorate and coordinate. In the highly conceptualized circumstance, a lowly peasant might find himself dressed all in white, because everyone in his pastoral segment of the play is conceived to be more genuine and unspoiled than the city dwellers whom we've seen dressed all in black. If a decorating costumer gets hold of this peasant, he's likely to wind up with a white-on-white patchwork vest trimmed in quaintly bobbling ball fringe and a jaunty cap perched upon his head with the invisible assistance of horsehair, fourteen bobby pins, and half a bottle of spirit gum.

It's very, very hard for a costume designer to make a character look ordinary. If someone is to have "bad taste," the temptation is to comment on that bad taste or overdo the bad taste to the point where the costume may become monolithic and unfairly over-shadow any subtlety in the actor's work. Comedy, of course, is the one genre in which overstatement is OK and even desirable. Some designers adore the opportunity for comedic exaggeration in cos-tume, as much as they may feel stifled by the subtleties of dramatic understatement or misdirection. Mysteries provide a designer with a similar chance to play with reasonably broad characterizations within a noncomedic context. No matter the genre — comedy, mystery, realistic kitchen-table play, allegorical fantasy, or sumptuous costume classic — careful discussion of a character's background and attitude should precede or inform all considerations of color, silhou-ette, and decoration. Character analysis must serve as the basis for every aesthetic choice. Costuming a human character versus a man-nequin separates theatrical design from fashion design. When the dictates of a character's age, social status, or psychological state are less important than showing off a designer's smashing 1950s research or tightly controlled color palette, life begins to leak from the edges of a production.

I'm not saying that you can't have it all: terrific research, glorious tonalities, and human plausibility. A designer needs to be a resourceful matchmaker, pairing details from her everyday observations and her research with a breakdown of each character's given circumstances, motivations, and moods. To that she adds alternate layers of inspiration, selectivity, and balance to bring the look of the play together as a whole. For me, it comes back again to working from the inside out, and in this process, the actor can be a crucial collaborator. A set may not have feelings about how it looks, but an actor does.

If a performer, who has done painstaking analysis to construct a believable internal life for his character, cannot recognize himself in the external façade foisted upon him by the costume designer, he will be less effective. Does anyone perform confidently or naturally at the prom? Well, maybe some do — those who harbor an inner prince or princess. Most people don't quite know who they're supposed to be in formal attire, but they can get away with it for one night. Onstage in front of an audience eight times a week, an actor has to be able to consistently and confidently embody his image. A performer relies on the costume designer to help him identify with his character. No, the clothes shouldn't look more expensive or tasteful than the character could afford or choose. They should be age-appropriate, unless the character is deluded in that respect. They should be place-appropriate, unless the character is an outsider or has recently moved. Most important, a costumer, an actor, and a director should agree upon the self-image that drives the character to affiliate himself or exclude himself from a recognizable category of dress. Creating a façade is an irresistible delight for any costumer. Inhabiting a façade may be an expanding adventure or a frustrating obstacle to an actor.

The moral is: If plans call for the wolf to show up onstage in sheep's clothing:

1. The costume designer better check out a lot of sheep.

2. The costume designer better find out how the wolf feels about his disguise.

3. The costume designer better ask the shepherd how the sheep see the wolf.

4. The costume designer better know if the audience is supposed to suspect anything from the wolf's looks. Or should they find out when he eats the sheep?

A costumer must know her characters. Whether, as in the case of the ingenue in white, the costume is supposed to reflect the innocence of her character, or in the case of the wolf, it masks his true nature and purpose, their clothes will be more interesting if the designer understands the relationship between the man and the image of the man.

Chapter Four

My Right Shoulder Is Slightly Higher Than My Left

WORKING WITH ACTORS

I have yet to meet the stunningly beautiful human who is completely at home in his or her body. Come to think of it, I've never met anyone who is. Socrates was definitely on to something when he posited the mind-body dichotomy. Most of us exist within a mechanism that is out to do us wrong at every turn. You get a week's vacation, and your back goes out packing the car. You spend way too much money on an outfit for that night of nights, and inevitably a large pimple appears on the tip of your nose. The majority of us have beautiful souls but rarely do we see them in the mirror.

My experience as a costume designer has encouraged me to stand behind another, less ancient philosophical premise: "I think, therefore I am." Surely Descartes was unaware of the generations of anorexic women who would live by this a priori truth — I think I am fat, therefore I am. Others bend the phrase to fit the body. I think I wear size thirty-two pants, therefore I do. I think I look bilious in earth tones, therefore I won't wear them (even if I am playing Pocahontas). I think my right shoulder is slightly higher than my left, therefore, *that* is the main focus of everyone's attention.

The fact that her mind and body may tend to work at cross purposes presents a particular challenge to a performer. An actor's body is her tool, her vehicle, her instrument. She expresses all things to all people. She embodies myriad fantasies. An actor cannot afford to sit at home in a bathrobe imagining what she might look like if she were to put down that kielbasa and join the gym. She has to get up in front of several hundred people every night and revel in however her body looks, feels, and works at that moment — not two days from now when her migraine goes away. Of all of us, actors can least allow themselves to be deluded about their physicality. By and large, my experience is that they don't.

For most performers, beauty, or the lack thereof, is part of their craft. Most have spent a good deal of time in front of their mirrors. Those with a good eye have learned early on which parts of their face or stature need remediation and which should be showcased. In countless auditions, they have honed the art of standing out from the crowd. To some degree (often to a large degree), actors are cast in plays for how they look. At best, their special "quality," a projection of spirit through physical presence, is desirable to the director, important to the overall vision of the play, and should *not* be discounted, obscured, or sabotaged by an obtuse costume designer.

From what I've seen, most performers have been burned by costume designers more often than they've been beautified. I know there are legendary alliances such as those between Audrey Hepburn and Hubert de Givenchy, Grace Kelly and Edith Head, Cher and Bob Mackie. How fortunate are those who find a brilliant designer to enhance and distinguish them. But for most non-superstars who have yet to immortalize a look or put a personal stylist on payroll, the experience of being costumed brings them back to the days when Mom picked out their clothes. Mom, in most cases, was not on their wavelength.

In conventional theater wisdom, "Everything looks better under lights." Actors, like the fabled Sarah Bernhardt, are said to have "stage faces." They transform from ugly ducklings on the street to resplendent swans when presented to an audience. Conversely, even if their faces look terrific, I have often seen actors who, at the hands of a costume designer, look worse on stage than in real life. Discounting the possibility that the character is, perhaps, supposed to look bad, the reasons are many: lack of budget, lack of time, inept cutter, inept wig person. These are reasons, but they're not good reasons. None of them is insurmountable. What's insurmountable is a costume designer who's not paying attention, who's insecure, defensive, indecisive, or inexperienced in the fitting room.

There are two distinct parts of a costume designer's job as it relates to an actor: drawing the sketch and working in the fitting room. As a student designer, I put the greatest part of my creative energy into improving my skills as a sketch artist. Most young designers do. As I emerged from graduate school and the protection of a nurturing, academic costume shop, I began to experience serious gaps in my ability to carry my best sketches forward to become equally successful costumes. While costume sketches are crucial to the preliminary design process, they are one-dimensional, linear forms, and costumes are actually three-dimensional, sculptural forms.

The art of the costume sketch is, in some ways, antagonistic to the sculptural process of the fitting. Designers often turn characters into generalized, paper-doll shapes as they necessarily turn out sketches at a fast rate. Simplified, schematic renderings have their merit, particularly in working out the geometry of a costume — the shape and proportion of the silhouette. More misleading are sketches, often slick and stylishly appealing, which have their basis in fashion illustration. The average human is reported to be eight heads high. Fashion designers routinely design on a body eleven heads high and, of course, supernaturally thin. Simplifying or elongating usually produces a version of apples and oranges. Your costume may be great for a banana, but how will it look on a pear?

These misconceptions happen all the time, and usually the actor gets blamed. "Well she has no chest! How can they expect me to make her look good in a 1950s evening gown?" "He's too short to carry off the shoulders in a 1940s suit." Such problems can be managed; check out Audrey Hepburn and Jimmy Cagney. A successful costume, as opposed to a successful costume sketch, must be adapted to a real body, not carried out in spite of one (or over a dead one). My best designs have been conceived from day one with a particular body (not necessarily a perfect body) in mind.

It's not always possible for designs to be postponed until after a play is cast, but that's the ideal. I will do my research before casting and talk to the director about theme and character, but rarely will I begin to sketch until the actors have signed a contract. If I don't know an actor cast in a play, I promptly set out to learn as much about her as possible. After all, Kathy Bates or Holly Hunter could be cast as Candida, but would they both look good in the same costume design? No. I first call the actor and ask about her body and its particulars: likes, dislikes, what works, what doesn't. Though sometimes cautious or astonished, rarely are actors shy about confiding in me. (Oddly, those who are resistant to my questioning or dismissive of having particular personal requirements often turn out to be the most difficult and finicky in the eventual fittings.) My reasoning is this: Most preferences, idiosyncrasies, or even obsessions are going to come out eventually in the fitting or rehearsal process. Why not confront them ahead of time and incorporate them into a fabulous specific design for that performer? Have I been lied to? Yes, but usually only white lies. My policy is always believe what someone says about his arm length, and rarely believe what he claims to be his waist measurement. A few inches here or there isn't really the point of our conversation, which is to establish a basis for communication, trust, comfort, and experimentation. Without those things going for you, your future in the fitting room and dress rehearsal is more likely to be fractious, and the eventual stage picture is less likely to be pretty.

Once I have an idea of what an actor believes he looks like, I try to get the "factual" data, specifically a head shot and measurements from the last theater where he performed (usually more reliable than those supplied by his agent). Only then do I start the process of combining my research with my imagination. In the early stages of design, making multiple sketches on a body roughly approximating that of the actual performer enables me to work out questions of scale and proportion before I'm in the fitting room with an actor and a cutter looking at me expectantly for decisive answers. I often show my rough sketches to the director and to the costume shop. If I know the actor fairly well, I may even send her some preliminary choices. The idea here is to get as much specific feedback early on when I'm in a position to do something about it rather than later when labor has gone into patterning, costly fabric has been cut, and time is running out. This may seem obvious, but I have seen designers so insecure about their preliminary sketches or so wary of interference that they refuse to show anyone anything less than a finished rendering. By so doing, they basically cut short the collaborative process. Directors are often too intimidated by a compelling sketch to voice a negative opinion. So much do they respect the artwork that they're hesitant to talk in prosaic terms about the character and the clothing. Reticent actors may have the same problem. Worried that there is something not right about a costume design, but respecting the artistry of the designer, they wait until later to make a protest when it's actually much harder to change the costume. This I know is true: It's easier to redraw a costume than to rebuild one.

In no way do I want to denigrate the importance or fascination of evocative costume sketches. Sketching is probably my favorite part of costume design, and I devote more time than necessary to the process. It is impossible for me to really integrate and balance the colors in a set of costumes unless I can work ahead of time, at the solitude of my desk, surrounded by swatches. Even more than many other designers, I come up with my most creative ideas pencil, rather than fabric, in hand. But a sketch is not the end of the design process. Ideas sometimes have to change to accommodate the cold, hard facts.

I have often noticed that actors seem to trust the cutters and stitchers in a shop more than they do the costume designer. One reason may be that the shop is focused on the costume itself, not on the sketch or the concept. Actors' problems are often practical rather than conceptual — I can't run up and down a staircase fifteen times in this hot woolen suit; I can't lift my arms high enough in these tight sleeves to do my love scene. Cutters and stitchers are eager, and often better equipped, to solve the technical difficulties of a garment. But any costume designer who turns her sketches over to the shop with the attitude "just make it happen" is really cutting herself out of the heart of the process. For me, the time spent by an actor and designer in the fitting room is hands down the most crucial factor in how the actor will look onstage.

In every fitting, at least three very different skills are required simultaneously. First of all, there's the aforementioned sculptural part of the job. In a fitting, the designer must wean himself from the fantasy of his sketch and confront the realities of fabric and form. What about that circular ruffle just below the hip? How does it look from the back, how about the sides? Should it angle down three inches below the hip or five inches? Which position is more flattering to the actor's shape? How does any change in ruffle placement relate to the balance of the silhouette as a whole? To make the ruffle work, should the feather on the hat be two inches shorter and the heels on the shoes two inches taller? Scale, balance, and proportion are on a designer's mind continually. In addition to making these aesthetic choices, a designer routinely involves herself in numerous technical decisions. Should the neck be finished with bias cording or a facing? How stiff does the petticoat need to be to support the weight of the skirt? Does the collar need wiggly bones? Should there be gussets under the arms? What are the fastenings? Does the costume need to be rigged for a quick change? Such construction issues become easier to answer with experience, and a designer can always ask for advice from the shop manager or cutter. Perhaps more demanding than the visual and structural aspects of a fitting is the psychological component.

Every human dynamic has its challenges. A costume fitting has to be up there with a first date or a job interview for instantaneous, artificial intimacy. By its very nature, a fitting is an invasion of personal space. The actor is the one physically vulnerable person in a room filled with anywhere from two to six fully clothed individuals. There's the designer, possibly the design assistant, the cutter, the first hand, and others who might include the shop manager, the wig maker, the craftsperson, or the dresser. The actor, undressed, in a mirrored room full of people concentrating on every oddity of his anatomy, is living what, for most of us, would be the stuff of minor nightmares. Generally inured to this humbling process, actors are invariably grateful to a costume designer who can infuse the atmosphere with good manners, humor, empathy, higher purpose, or some combination thereof.

A costume designer's behavior toward a performer sets the tone for the entire fitting. Though humor is important and goes a long way toward lessening an actor's self-consciousness and a designer's obsessiveness, it is extremely detrimental if set on the loose. Costume technicians, used to spending long hours together with only the dummies to listen, often develop a form of gallows banter. Even a stray remark about the odd perversity of a separating zipper that wouldn't go into its boned bodice could make an actor permanently insecure about her costume. The theater is full of superstitious folks, and nobody wants to be stuck in a jinxed bodice with a jinxed zipper — rest assured that sucker will break on stage. Worse yet is to match wits with an actor who is mocking himself. Never does that lead to fun. I have learned to ignore any possible opening for feeding a performer's self-doubt or second-guessing. I would not really call myself a wildly positive person. Certainly, I'm more comfortable operating from a skeptical position in the gray zone. Not so in a fitting. In a fitting, my ideal vision is queen. I always look at the positive aspects of each person and am determined to live up to them. Believe it or not, this attitude is surprisingly workable and, best of all, infectious. There's really no one who can't look great in clothes. But a facile designer has to see past the problems, forget preconceptions, and work quickly and intuitively with what she really sees before her.

One important thing to figure out ASAP is what an actor can "carry off." We all know this about ourselves and each other to some degree. One person can carry off a hat. (My daughter can, I can't, so it's not a dominant gene.) Another can carry off a cape — let's hope he's the guy chosen to play Dracula. Some women love a train; others fight every inch of one and rarely win. There are women dying to show cleavage and others who don't want to be bothered with the distraction. Many actors like a very tight waistband; others are miserable with any physical restriction. Leg o' mutton sleeves? Hedda Gabler better be bigger than they are, or you've got one foolish-looking heroine.

Some designers and many directors believe that carrying off a costume can be taught. They're kind of like behavioral psychologists. It would be preposterous for me to state that a person is born with the knack to wear clothes. But I do know that if someone has taught an individual to be a clotheshorse, it wasn't me. I can tell an actor until I'm blue in the face that the way to move with a train is to walk *around* it. Never turn abruptly right or left; pretend there's a large Doric column on either side of you and circle it. It makes no difference. If the person doesn't possess the inner rhythm conducive to a measured, stately gait, she'll end up flicking the train behind her with a petulant kick or, even more unseemly, will sometimes haul the train up over one arm and stride around like a Roman senator in a toga. Actually, let's not even discuss togas. (Three out of five actors are helpless in those esoteric draperies.)

When you finally do get to design a Renaissance Shakespeare, what a rude awakening to find that not every man is a Laurence Olivier, or even a Leonard Whiting. Tights and pumpkin hose require major carrying-off ability. I vividly remember a production of *The Tempest* for which I had my first really hefty Shakespearean budget. Ferdinand was, as yet, a minor actor but a major clothes-horse. He looked so great in his Dureresque costume that hearts melted as soon as he hit the stage. Unfortunately, he did just that. His boyish exuberance prompted him to leap from a lofty part of the steeply raked set and badly sprain an ankle. A replacement Ferdinand was flown in, and although his measurements were very similar, his tights-wearing ability was not. Now, this replacement was an excellent actor, and even book-in-hand, he spoke Ferdinand's lines with a lyrical intensity our Miranda had never before enjoyed. But, he simply looked ridiculous in the rather flashy costume designed to showcase a very different set of calves on a very different ego. So, in the end, would I rather costume a clotheshorse or a terrific actor? (As Jack Benny would say, "I'm thinking about it.") No, the satisfaction of a production in which people look better than they act is short-lived and self-defeating. The point is, Ferdinand number two would never have made it past the first fitting in my original costume design. I would have seen that he couldn't carry it off, and the costume would have metamorphosed. He might have ended up with thigh-high boots rather than revealing tights. Perhaps he was a cape person. I never had the time to discover his sartorial strengths.

Time, of course, is what there's always not enough of in theater. Having worked over fifteen years for one regional theater with a resident company, I have learned tremendous secrets by costuming the same actors repeatedly. When I first arrived to take my resident design position, I was in my early thirties with enough experience to be fairly sure of myself. What a shock to encounter a stable of old pros, some of whom had been wearing costumes literally before I was born. Initially, the company was fairly wary of me. They had been fortunate to work for many years with an excellent costume designer who had been a friend and inspiration to all. In the year between his departure and my arrival, they had been subjected to a designer, fresh out of graduate school, who knew nothing about costume construction. Though undeniably creative and not to be deterred, my immediate predecessor had conceived a string of ornate and unworkable getups in which many of the actors felt lost and humiliated. Their most horrific stories included a production of *Julius Caesar* in which they wore football shoulder pads and helmets for armor.

My first fittings with these new colleagues were uncomfortable, to say the least. Several company members told me, point blank, what they would and would not wear; they didn't care how nice my watercolor technique might be. I was forced into an improvisational mode, and though time was short and not every compromise resulted in a smashing costume, I had to admit that the actors looked better in their modified costumes than they would have in my original designs. Since that time, I have worked with many of those actors again and again. Inevitably, their costumes are the most successful in every production for four simple reasons: I know their bodies, I know how they move, I care about their feelings, and I respect their acting. Working up the same knowledge and regard for an unfamiliar actor during a four-week rehearsal period isn't easy. It can and must be accomplished, but it requires open eyes and an open mind.

Because time is literally money when working with equity actors with whom a limited number of fittings are legally allowed, a costume designer, by necessity, shies away from open-ended, trial-and- error fitting situations. Particularly when a shop is building the majority of clothes for a large period production, patterning what might be thirty to fifty complete costumes usually precedes the average four- week rehearsal period in order to get the workload finished by opening night. In such highly pressured circumstances, a designer must commit to many decisions about each garment before ever setting eyes on the human who will wear it. But in smaller productions, for which construction may begin during the first week of rehearsal, or when some or all of the clothes are being bought or pulled from stock, I try to call a kind of exploratory fitting within the first few days of rehearsal. For this session, I pull various types of garments to see what best suits the actor's shape, movement, and temperament. Necessarily, I work ahead, measuring carefully and evaluating the ramifications of each look, to have only workable possibilities on hand. Each choice might represent a very different approach to the character, but I have to be able to live with any of the choices and any of them should be able to work with the rest of the clothes in that production. Without careful selection, a performer will likely bond with just the item that wasn't really a serious option; I'll start carping and our mutual comfort level will begin to disintegrate. Once a designer has witnessed, firsthand, how an actor looks and behaves in a variety of garments, she can much better shop, pull, or oversee a muslin mock-up for a built costume. Even if few or none of the garments tried in this first encounter is ever seen onstage, the time, if at all available, will have been well spent. Actors seldom begrudge the attention.

One final event in the fitting process marks the ultimate success of any costume. Sometimes it comes in the first fitting, sometimes not until the final dress rehearsal: the moment when I recognize the character. It always hits me like a welcome ton of bricks, and usually everyone in the fitting room sees it at the same time. The actor may simply unbutton a button or turn up a collar. He may try on the tenth hat or the sixth pair of shoes. I may throw a shawl across her shoulders or hand her a pair of glasses. Many times, of course, it's when the wig is finished or the basting threads have been pulled after a final pressing. At that moment the character comes alive, and the fitting is no longer really about the actor.

One of my favorite character-defining moments came in a fitting with the actor Delroy Lindo. The play, *The Black Branch* by Gary Leon Hill, called for Delroy's character to wear a burn mask, obscuring most of his very expressive features. We had been through a few fittings and had settled on the clothes. Delroy was wearing an old white T-shirt, a pair of loose, vintage, linen pants, and some worn yellow suspenders. As Delroy stood in front of the mirror he quietly said, "I think he'd just wear these backwards." He proceeded to turn his pants around so that they zipped behind him, rear pockets hanging perversely below his stomach and the Y shape of the suspenders falling in front, across his chest. This peculiar change made him look like a twisted, broken marionette and was perfectly expressive of the odd character he was to become. Such transformational moments are pure magic. They're part of an entire evolution specific to theatrical design. Words become drawings and the drawings become living, breathing, three-dimensional realities. If the angels all arrive on the head of the pin, you get the proprietary pleasure of seeing a whole cast of these creations onstage, performing a magnificent play.

So what about that obsessive performer who can't see past her right shoulder? I say pad the left shoulder; put a rose on it. I do whatever I can, creatively, to alleviate important insecurities, and then I celebrate that which is secure. Never will a designer come off well by calling attention to the fact that an actor may not be physically perfect for a role. Concentrating on what makes an actor gorgeous is absorbing and genuinely rewarding. No one has the body he really deserves. That's why I have a job. Any costume designer worth her title should be able to contrive the means to glorify that which nature and the casting director have provided.

Chapter Five

The Hierarchy of Theater

KNOWING WHERE YOU STAND

Anyone set on having his own way should not be a costume designer. Though arguably an artist, a costume designer can ill afford the classic artistic temperament. He is not the type to struggle alone in his garret, developing an autonomous, iconoclastic vision. Autonomy is the last thing he is likely to achieve, nor in fact, would he be well suited to it. A costume designer is a hive person, one who instinctively likes order imposed from above and happily passes on more work to those laboring below. A costume designer does not want to stop the buck. Yes, he must make decisions. Yes, he must be creative. He has lots of problems to solve and is inspired to do so beautifully and thematically. He may get carried away with a bizarre concept, but the hive-bound costume designer is ever mindful that he must accomplish his goal with the labor available, in the time available, with the money available, on the bodies available.

The economic principle of scarcity rules the theater, a place where ideas are usually bigger than budgets, talent is invariably greater than salary, and the workload is always larger than the labor force. By necessity, the synergy of the whole must be greater than the sum of its parts. Under the pressure of immovable deadlines, a group of disparate, "alternative" personalities must get acquainted quickly and work together productively. Collaboration, a word much tossed about when discussing theater, sounds so deceptively chummy and unstructured. A theater may be a chummy place (at least histrionically so), but to facilitate a speedy and sometimes blessedly temporary interdependence, it's a highly structured one. The theater is egalitarian only insomuch as everyone has an equal opportunity to quit. Behind any theatrical enterprise exists a rigid human hierarchy. The balance of power within this pecking order may vary slightly according to the talents, desires, and numbers of its participants, but there will always be one. In the words of George Orwell, "All animals are equal but some are more equal than others."

The following diagram attempts to schematize a production hierarchy. This setup might exist within a typical independent theater, overseen by a board of directors, funded by a combination of federal, state, corporate, and private sponsors. Parallel to, and sometimes intersecting this artistic order, would be another management/business hierarchy. In the diagram, I am assuming the play has been written, the dramaturg has spoken, cuts have been made, and the playwright is either dead or out of town. Granted, this entire breakdown is seen from a costume designer's vantage point — and she's stuck in the middle with a somewhat obstructed view.

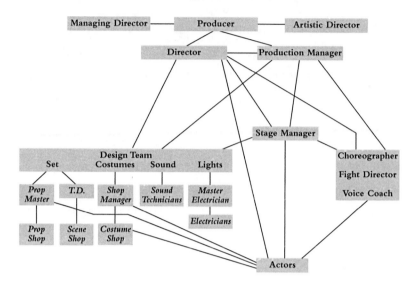

At the high-clout end of the labor schema is the producer. This personage is usually more than one human: a managing director and an artistic or producing director. Both ultimately report to the board of directors. The managing directors' ongoing concerns are fund-raising; managing the staff, the money, and the building; and selling tickets. A costume designer may not ever speak a word to the managing director, but he looms over her as the great and powerful keeper of the budget. The artistic/producing director may and probably does involve herself with fund-raising, possibly keeps abreast of staff concerns, and follows ticket sales. In her actual artistic role, she chooses the plays for each season, selects the directors and designers for every production, has final say in casting, and may oversee the aesthetic choices made by each production team, consisting of a director, possibly a dramaturg, as well as the set, costume, lighting, and sound designers. Depending on the artistic director's personality or schedule, the costume designer will encounter her at production meetings and rehearsals frequently, occasionally, or never.

The production manager is the main intermediary between the costume designer and the higher beings (the artistic and managing directors). Though the actual power to hire and fire, give money or take it away, reject ideas or embrace them rests with the artistic and managing directors, the production manager carries the good and bad news back and forth and up and down. The production manager makes sure all the stage-bound gears, including stage management, design, construction, acting and backstage crews, are moving in a synchronized manner.

Every play is brought to the stage by the efforts of a production team. The production team operates as a sort of duchy within the kingdom of the producing organization. The duke, who shall henceforth be known to us as the director, holds sway over a considerable number of lesser beings — though he pays homage to the artistic and managing directors, and if he knows what's good for him, will pay court to the production manager. Unless the artistic director is taking on a pet project and directing a play herself, the director is a hired gun. He has no say concerning the theater's overall artistic policy and little say concerning money. In most circumstances, the director is given a choice as to his designers and will usually opt for someone he knows or has heard about, or whose portfolio has managed to intrigue him. He oversees all design work: reviews and selects the research, selects the period in which the play will be set, OKs the ground plan, accepts or rejects the set model and costume sketches, dictates the mood of the lights, and approves every sound cue. With the help of a casting director and the approval of the artistic director, he auditions and casts the actors for his production. In rehearsal, the director decides how and where the actors will move onstage. If the actors are to perform back handsprings dressed in cartwheel farthingales and peascod bellies, it's the director's right to say it will be so and to tell the choreographer and costume designer to work out the details between them. The director has final say over what motivates each actor and how he will react to that motivation. Does Gertrude know the goblet offered by Claudius to Hamlet is poisoned? Is she a suicide or a pawn? It's the director's call, not Gertrude's (unless Gertrude is an actor of major reputation). For a brief, four- to six-week period, the director is Father, Mother, God, and Country to every member of the cast and crew, and it is everyone's earnest wish to please him.

Why is this so? In a word: charisma. Directors have *it*. Good directors are among the most charming, intelligent, inventive, and undauntable creatures you'll ever want to meet. They possess in abundance what Robert Edmond Jones termed "The Dramatic Imagination." Of course, all members of a production team must have their fair share of dramatic imagination, but many can't stand the heat generated by the process of bringing ideas to life. The number of people and problems each member of the production team can handle while simultaneously defending his dramatic vision in large part ordains his position in the production hierarchy. A director is willing to go out on the highest limb for the best ideas — and once she's out there on that limb, she is enthusiastic and assertive enough to coax all others to join her, or at least climb somewhere up on the tree. The director combines a multitude of aesthetic and political skills. She's instinctively open-minded, but she has impeccable and very specific taste. She's seemingly free of the strangling tendency to self-edit, yet, when it comes down to the wire, she knows what part of the production must go, what must stay, and what needs to be rearranged. She is sensitive to the process of her cohorts, yet is terse and unafraid of command. She has vision, yet she is never bored by nit-picking detail. One director may not possess all of these qualities, but she will have some other equally engaging, amusing, fascinating, or seductive combination of traits that will ignite the talents of those around her.

With the director on the backstage, pre-rehearsal planning side of a production is the design team, basically comprising the set, costume, lighting, and sound designers. Each member of that team may be near or far from the director's decision-making process depending on his history of work with the director, his knowledge of the theater or producing organization, his experience with the performers or "the star," his stature in the profession, or his aptitude for the project. Pre-rehearsal interaction among the designers themselves and between each designer and the director varies according to the technical requirements of the play and the loquaciousness of the individuals.

The set designer lays out the physical environment of the play, dictating where and how the actors may move. In film, there is generally an overall production designer, though I have never run into one in the theater. Instead, the set designer of a play is occasionally understood to be the orchestrating designer. This is most often the case with a master designer, a Ming Cho Lee or John Conklin, who is fully capable of designing every aspect of a production but chooses to handle only the sets while working closely with compatible lighting and costume designers. In any case, set designers are most often responsible for coming up with what is said to be the *visual metaphor* for a play. Their decisions set the style, tone perspective, and movement of a production. The set designer is very often the first to meet with the director (in some cases with the director and the dramaturg). In more expansively collaborative situations, one or more of the other designers are included from the beginning, as well.

The lighting designer will, quite naturally, influence the set design and, in turn, be influenced by it. Changes of light will alter the atmosphere of a production and so affect the selective view, the mood, and the temporal progression of a set. The lighting designer's work also intersects with that of the costume designer, in large part because the colors of her lights will affect the appearance of color on the costumes. Numerous arcane technical aspects of the lighting designer's trade may set her apart from the set and costume designers in relationship with the director. Anyone feels capable of discussing a door, a platform, a top hat, or a three-piece suit; few chat fluently on the subject of beam angles. The set designer can or should talk the lighting designer's language, the sound designer probably will, the costume designer may. It's up to the lighting designer to decide if she is interested in crossing over from her technical side of the river to involve herself with the other designers and the director in early thematic and research discussions. Some enjoy it, some don't.

Sound designers interact indirectly with set, costume, and lighting designers. Often a sound designer will participate in early, conceptual discussions, but his work, being less tangible and requiring fewer hands to manufacture than that of the set and costume designer, allows him a greater level of independence and flexibility. He frequently works one on one with the director, selecting music and sounds that will be tested throughout the rehearsal process. Emotionally and stylistically, his work may interest the other members of the design team and vice versa, but being aural rather than visual, it doesn't physically overlap theirs.

A costume designer's placement in the theatrical design hierarchy, and more specifically her position relative to that of the set designer, is analogous to the status of fashion designers versus that of architects. Architecture, because of its size, the formidable materials and labor required for its construction, and the scope of its influence on human action, imposes itself with greater consequence than does its more personal, flimsy, and evanescent sister fashion. Architecture is positioned adjacent to art upon the summit of high culture, while couture lives one or two steps down, in the world of popular culture. Yes, art museums have come to acknowledge fashion, or rather cash in on its drawing power. Turnouts for popular exhibits at the Met's Costume Institute often outstrip those for more prestigious fine art displays. But fashion, with its inevitable link to human utility and personality, has traditionally been considered, like furniture, a decorative art.

Because of this connection, a theatrical costume designer has as much if not more in common with the property master (who supplies the furnishings and decorations for the set as well as any items touched but not worn by the actors) as she does with the set designer. Though the set designer will usually design or select most of the furniture and props, it is the property master who, when necessary, instructs the actors in their function and use. The costume designer maintains no such distance from the actors. More than any member of the design team, her work is inextricably linked to them. Individual humans demand so much more say than do empty theater spaces. This human element of personality and utility sullies costuming in terms of pure, conceptual design. Costumers, in their role as pragmatic facilitators are often down in the trenches, while set designers maintain their distance on a more elevated, abstract plain.

Whatever his traditional position on the design team, the costume designer is undeniably influential to a production. He may first stimulate the curiosity and respect of the director and set designer by the quality and novelty of his research. Since fashion changes more rapidly than does architecture, costumes are crucial to defining the period in which a play is set. Costumes can make or break the color palette of a production so, in that area, close agreement between designers benefits all. Whether the costume designer is called upon to give opinions as to the final set, lighting, or sound designs depends on his intelligence, taste, and tact, though giving such opinions would never be considered his inalienable right.

There are unique teams of directors and designers who in no way conform to this traditional hierarchy. Darron West, a tremendously talented and gregarious sound designer, works so closely with the director Anne Bogart and her company, he is rarely absent from a day's rehearsal. He is as fully present to the creative process as is every performer. His sound informs the space, the rhythms, the color, and countless other aspects of a SITI performance. The director Robert Wilson is his own production designer, usually conceiving the sets and working carefully with other master designers to costume and light his strongly imagistic performances. Julie Taymor directs and also designs her own costumes and puppets. In dance companies, lighting designers and costume designers often form the core design team, since sets are less dominant. The balance of power may rearrange itself among designers, the more the scope of their abilities becomes familiar.

As directors and designers work repeatedly together, the process of taking a play "from the page to the stage" inevitably becomes more interactive and less hierarchical. When designers know and trust and, more important, excite and complement one another, working together is freeing and even intoxicating. I've often marveled at the magical nature of drawing. Surprising things flow from my pencil, usually after a series of false starts or clumsy approximations. That same mysterious energy, almost like an incantation, may burst forth in early designer/director discussions. One idea sparks another, and together, a series of deeply moving conceptions emerge. The social nature of creativity in the theater is strongly addicting.

Once the costume and set designs have been approved and re-hearsals get underway, the theatrical hierarchy branches out and in-tertwines. The director is still sovereign, but the stage manager, the actors, and the production shops begin the task of transforming a se-ries of ideas and drawings into an actual performance.

The stage manager becomes the single most important link be-tween all participants in production and performance. She functions within the duchy created to mount a specific play much as the pro-duction manager does in the theater at large. She is actually in close touch with the production manager, keeping the higher echelons in-formed about her play's progress. The stage manager records every decision made in every rehearsal. She relates pertinent information on a daily basis to every member of the design and production teams. She arranges meetings with the director and between the de-signers, choreographer, fight coordinator, music director, voice coach, flying specialists, and so on. She schedules costume fittings and organizes the use of props. You name the job, a great stage man-ager knows every detail involved and how each detail will impact other, seemingly unrelated, aspects of the work as a whole. A great stage manager knows which of the two Pigeon Sisters in *The Odd Couple* carries the shoulder-strap bag, which has the clutch, and how said handbags will affect their blocking. If an actor pulls a handker-chief out of his pocket during a rehearsal, the costume designer, the wardrobe crew, and the costume shop will receive notes from the stage manager. "Algernon needs a handkerchief in the muffin scene. Are there pockets in his act 2 Norfolk Jacket?" Communication and good relations with the stage manager are a *must* for anyone in the production hierarchy. Because she knows everything and everyone — the dresser doing a thirty-second fast change offstage right, the sound technician waiting for his cue in the booth, the actor watching backstage left for his entrance light, and the director expecting to see the final blackout fourteen seconds after Fortinbras's last line — everyone is at her mercy. The stage manager is the Rasputin or the Merlin of a production, depending on your luck.

As the nuts-and-bolts (or hooks-and-eyes) work of the production shops moves into action, each designer begins a completely new phase of her job, requiring her to flex different social muscles from those she formerly has used to interact with the director and design team. A costume designer, while protected from some of the responsibilities of high command, must nonetheless demonstrate leadership skills in dealing with the costume shop. She is responsible for delivering on the promises of her costume sketches, and although she's not exactly the boss of the costume shop, she must engender some respect or at least inspire enough enthusiasm to get the job done. In the case of Broadway and some Off Broadway productions, a costume designer may cast a deciding vote as to what costume shop will be contracted to do the work, but in nonprofit regional theater, the shop is a given, and the designer is essentially a jobber.

Demonstrating skills closely resembling those of a well-connected snake oil salesman, the costume designer must hustle to win over the shop to her grand scheme. Considerable effort and good will is required of those who are to transform a bunch of whimsical doodles into one-of-a-kind structures made of fabric, buckram, feathers, and faux fur, that additionally must be comfortable, flattering, durable, easy to get on and off — and beautiful, let's not forget that. At her best, a costume designer is one part Scheherazade, in her ability to intrigue and delight, and one part Queen Elizabeth I, in her capacity to stay the course while commanding some degree of deference and regard. Chief accessories to her efforts are her costume sketches, which serve not only to pass on information but also to garner the enthusiasm and incite the creative juices of the costume shop. A costume designer's research, the organization of her materials, her ability to think on her feet and, most important, her willingness to make decisions will decide the success of her relationship with those on whom she depends to carry out her designs.

The diagram below shows the basic pecking order of a costume shop. The number of individuals varies widely from theater to theater and production to production. For example, there may be as many as three or four teams, consisting of a cutter, a first hand, and one or two stitchers, on a large Shakespearean production or a musical. There may be more than one shopper or a resident design assistant and a shopper. Sometimes there is only one craftsperson, sometimes several. No matter what the exact staffing of a costume shop, their universal feature is that the crew — though generally skilled, well educated, intelligent, and hard working — are underestimated and undercompensated by the administration. I have never encountered a costume shop whose staff salaries are as high as those of the scene shop in the same theater, even though their skills and workload are absolutely on a par. Perhaps this disparity trickles down from the pay gap between set designers and costume designers; their salaries are historically unequal, even though they belong to the same union and work in the same venues. This explains, to some degree, why in the costume shop (kissing cousin to the sweatshop,

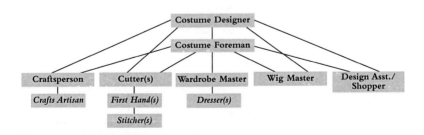

which supposedly no longer exists in this country) disgruntlement and insurrection usually lurk just below the surface, no matter how smooth the waters may appear. The costume designer must navigate these troubled seas, so her livelihood depends on the perpetuation of an inherently politically incorrect situation. (But what the hell, theater itself is not exactly a socialist utopia, or even a Jeffersonian democracy.) Most often, the costume workers are so internally motivated, proud, and even altruistic that they do their best, no matter what the circumstance. But a costume designer never knows what show has just preceded hers, what will follow, what dynamics have developed among the staff, and how close to the breaking point everyone has been driven. It behooves her, by at least day two, to make speedy adjustments to everyone's personality, energy level, and skill if she is to get them on her side — that is, the side of her precise vision and level of perfectionism versus the side of just getting the work done.

The designer's most substantive and particular interactions involve the cutters, also called drapers. They are undoubtedly the most crucial and rare talents in the shop. Costume designers, in fact, are easier to come by than cutters, so that makes it clear from the beginning (no matter what their relative positions on the hierarchy of command) who's really got the upper hand. Very few schools train cutters. They most often work their way up through the costume ranks by dint of God-given ability and years of experience. Like many fine craftsmen, they are usually so shy, nonpolitical, or wrapped up in their work that they are the last to speak up for themselves — they let the costume designer do that for them, hence the costume designer often gets credit for their genius. Cutters are responsible for turning a designer's sketch into a costume, and that takes a great deal of discernment and ingenuity. What seems like a clear decision to a designer may look like an errant pencil squiggle to anyone but a hawk-eyed cutter. For architectural drawings, there are certain conventions and scale rule exactitudes that a builder can go by. A draper reading a costume sketch has to interpret a much less codified series of hieroglyphics. There are at least five ways to cut an 1890s skirt. Your draper has to choose the right one to make moving fabric, on a real, live woman, look as magical as your impressionistic, two-dimensional drawing. Small decisions as to placement of bias and straight grain, darting, seaming, and matching of patterns can make a big difference in how the final garment will look and move. A good cutter asks the right questions, understands the research, and rarest of all, has a "good hand." She is a sculptor. Ideally, the cutters are heaven-sent creatures who make any designer look ten times better than he really is, and I am very lucky to have had this be the case in innumerable situations.

The costume designer is equally dependent on the work of the costume craftsperson. Anything worn by the actor but not actually considered clothing is apt to be thrown in the craftsperson's lap. This includes hats, shoes, and belts, for starters. Undergarments usually remain under a cutter's supervision, unless we're talking about giant farthingales and panniers, which might need the cooperation of the craftsperson for wire snipping and welding. Fabric treatments, such as dyeing, painting, and printing, which must be finished before a garment is cut, are also the job of the craftsperson. Trim, embroidery, or applique might be a craft job, or they might be a sewing job, depending on the shop. Aging costumes after they are built or purchased is a craft job requiring a particular degree of fine-tuning. Because the craftsperson's work is crucial to the ostensibly artistic look of the costumes, the costume designer works very closely with him and, again, must quickly get on his wavelength. How artificial or painterly the aging of the costumes should appear, how loosely or how precisely the hand-painted fabrics should be rendered, how much blue dye or how much red is used to create the purple fabric — all affect the final look of the clothes. Every craftsperson has an individual style, and the costume designer must try to coordinate that style with her own. Millinery is a case in point, every hat being a one-of-a-kind masterpiece. Even if a designer provides working drawings, showing front, back, right-side, left-side, and top views, there are still decisions about scale and construction that will affect the final look of a hat. If a costumer is lucky, the craftsperson will like the designs, enjoy the materials, and contribute his own good judgment, experience, and creativity to the cause.

Eventually, the costume designer depends on the kindness of every member of the costume crew. The costume shop manager helps her to keep abreast of budget and labor dilemmas as well as scheduling needs. She will be on hand to help the designer through weekend technical rehearsals, or she will be mysteriously called away, depending on how much credit and affection the designer has accumulated during the construction process. The shoppers will either go to six western outlet stores in three counties looking for the perfect size 14EEE snakeskin cowboy boots, or they will give up after two trips and order boring, unembellished cowhide ones from an online catalogue, depending on how urgently and convincingly the designer has put her specific wishes across. As a rule, the wardrobe crew will make fast changes work and keep costumes looking good just because they're loyal to the actors and don't want to let them down. But if it comes to a choice between an actor who doesn't really want to wear his coat and hat in act 3 and a costume designer who wants him to, the wardrobe mistress and dressers better have some rooting interest in the costume designer's good judgment, or they'll simply back the actor. "Sorry, we can't get that hat and coat over to stage right because he took it off earlier when he exited stage left and no one's available to retrieve it and reset it for act 3." What are you going to do? Show up every night and put the coat on him yourself? I don't think so, even if the wardrobe union would allow it.

So the costume shop and the costume designer have a delicately balanced symbiotic relationship. Each is dependent on the other to show off his talents, and each is vulnerable to the other's ineptitudes. The designer depends on the shop to make the clothes look fantastic according to her lights and to adapt to unforeseen changes. The shop depends on the designer to be prepared, to make good decisions in a timely manner, to handle the director's and actors' wishes and opinions, and to prevent costly mistakes and revisions if at all possible. If the designer is behind on her research or shopping, if she hasn't thought through the consequences of the wig design to the hat design or of the fabric treatment to the construction of the garment, or if she is just plain indecisive, she can make life very miserable for the costume crew, who, in the best of circumstances, have inadequate time to get their work done.

I have made design mistakes whose implications have had little impact on me but major impact on the costume shop. In a production of *The Tempest*, I coordinated the costume color palette for the allied Neapolitan Court of Duke Alonzo and the Milanese Court of Antonio, Prospero's usurping brother, to range from burgundies and grays through rusts and browns. The aged Gonzalo, though a councilor in the Neapolitan Court, was, according to the text, "honest" and had shown kindness to Prospero and Miranda upon Prospero's banishment. Mistakenly trying to project Gonzalo's lack of complicity with Prospero's enemies onto his costume, I robed him in green. In the first technical rehearsal, the director and the design team agreed that Gonzalo's unique coloration made him appear too important and distracted from the appropriate visual focus in certain scenes. For me to choose a new shade of velvet was not very difficult. For the shop to rebuy, recut, restitch, and retrim a new robe and hat in forty-eight hours was a major chore. They could easily have stonewalled me. It was my fault. They might have refused to work overtime or to find extra money in the supply budget to buy new materials. The production manager and managing director would, no doubt, have been sympathetic to them. Luckily for me, the costume shop was excited by the production. They loved the set by Ming Cho Lee and were much appreciated by the actors, who also liked their costumes. The cutter and milliner were ready to reconstruct Gonzalo's costumes before I had to ask.

Changes to the costume designs inevitably do occur during the rehearsal process. Some are at the behest of the designer, and if she's good enough or fortunate enough, she can push them through the shop. More difficult for the designer are changes foisted upon her when her heart isn't in them. Then the job of convincing the costume shop that unanticipated work is necessary is even less fun. For example, a fight director could insist that some part of Mercutio's sleeves inhibits his ability to duel. Since fight directors and costume designers are roughly on the same latitude in the hierarchy of command, the director must decide which element is more important, the elaborate Renaissance sleeves or the swashbuckle. In another case, an actor stops dead in the middle of a frantic chase scene to proclaim that the beaded trim on her period dress is catching on the curtain fringe as she climbs through the window. Will the trim be removed, will the curtains be drawn back, or will the director reblock? Depends on whether the actor is really trying to do the window bit or get out of it, how much the set designer loves the hang of the drapes, and whether the costume designer can make a compelling case that removal of the offending trim will destroy the underlying silk chiffon. In any case, whoever wins, costume designer, choreographer, set designer, actor, or director, someone in the technical department usually loses. It's up to a designer, happy or not, to make sure the final command is carried out. Paul Owen, resident set designer at Actors Theatre of Louisville for the past thirty years, routinely refers to the craftspeople in his shop as "the troops." Indeed, the loyalty of the technical director, props master, scene painter, et al. to Paul's unique and meticulous vision is similar to that which must be felt for a much-respected general.

Like any organization examined in cross section, the theater is a complex interactive network in which exists a high degree of specialization. I once heard General Wesley Clarke, supreme commander of NATO forces during the Kosovo conflict, state the job of any soldier, from general to private: "To know his duty and to perform it." That, in a nutshell, describes the work of anyone in the theater. Is a costume designer's duty set in stone? Yes, if you're talking about the upper end of the chain of command, it's relatively set. If you're talking about the lower end, down where grommets are grommeted and corsets are laced tight, there may be some flexibility. In other words, I have rarely been called upon to block a play, but I have draped skirts, painted fabric, and scoured thrift stores. Like a career officer, the knowledge of my duty and my maturing ability to perform it are a comfort to me. I have experimented with work "on the outside," but I am always drawn back to some theatrical hive. Every new theater has its own personality, but once I find my way back to the costume shop, I'm usually on familiar turf.

Whether or not an artist is autonomous, she functions in a world that makes practical demands upon her. For a theatrical designer, the buffer of collective creativity is intrinsically valuable. Motivation must always exist in equal parts with talent. Isolation inspires one creative energy; interaction fosters another.

A costume designer's ego must thrive outside the bright lights. Her work will seldom be mentioned in a review. Her name will be best known to other theatrical designers. Her costumes will rarely be the focal point of any production. One of the last compliments I like to hear is, "The costumes were fantastic but the play was really boring." That by no means makes me the winner. It's much more thrilling when people come out raving about a play and incidentally tell me my costumes were a great part of it. Does that make my ego different than Julian Schnabel's? Yes. Am I more modest? No. I can stand only so much heat and so much personal attention. Don't look for a costume designer on opening night. You probably won't find him. Most likely that's when he'll be on his own, probably working on his next project.

Chapter Six

Will the Play Survive the Concept?

DESIGN INTERPRETATION

This month, I will have the pleasure of seeing three Shakespearean plays within as many weeks, one of which has been directed by Peter Brook. I vividly remember Brook's 1970 production of *A Midsummer Night's Dream* in which the play was stripped of its usual flora and fauna and starkly set against a curved white wall. There, sitting with my parents in the Brooklyn Academy of Music, I experienced my first production concept. Not two years later, as a graduate student I would use the term *concept* at least three times a day. We conceptualized the daylights out of every class project. My theatrical fantasy for *Alice in Wonderland* featured all the characters costumed as

71

pieces of Victorian furniture, based on the concept that Alice's
dream was a reaction to the overwrought home decoration of her
time. One of my cohorts worked with a faculty director to formu-
late the concept of "blue cheese" for their production of *Ghost
Sonata*. Wow! Her costumes were all cheeseclothy, and veined with
dye, and kind of falling apart. They did everything short of reek.
What this all had to do with Strindberg I can't recall. These days if
and when someone utters the word *concept,* adrenaline flushes into
my system. "What is our concept for "The Scottish Play" — Kilts?
Pelts? Futuristic? Clinton White House? The fight-or-flight response
is instantly engaged. It's not that I recoil from an overarching the-
matic/imagistic approach for each production. Not at all. But I will
fight for a concept that fosters and identifies the ideas in a play, and
I will fly from one that confuses or subsumes them.

Concept, I guess, is a more pretentious term for the fact that plays
have to be taken to heart by those who produce them. Like a piece
of music, a play is subject to interpretation. With each passing year,
decade, or century, a play is reevaluated and redefined by the directors, dramaturgs, designers, and actors who stage it. Every time I read
a play, I'm struck by the life force lying dormant within its pages.
Like a genie released from its bottle, the import of a play is subject
to the whims of its new masters. Their insights, their life experience,
their present emotions determine the form and scope of the play's
potent magic. Their concept, good or bad, acts as a filter between the
play and the audience. This filter is a theatricalized (an acted, costumed, staged, lighted, and scored) version of their interpretation of
a play's situation or message. In other words, the production team
and the actors pick the time, place, textures, sounds, shapes, and
movements that, to them, best make sense as a backdrop for a play's
dramatic events. Whether their interpretive efforts are subtle or ob-

vious, innovative or trite, the audience and the play are at their mercy. "You will now see *A Midsummer Night's Dream* enacted for the umpteenth time as an Elizabethan *Hair*: a culture clash between the psychedelic hippies in the woods and the straights in Athens." The concept, in this case, is supposed to help the audience find connections between their own times and those of Shakespeare. "Don't be fooled by Middle English, we're a bunch of good-time folks like yourselves; some of us are short, some tall. We're just looking for love in all the wrong places." Does this concept reinvigorate the ideas of Shakespeare or diminish them?

I heard Sharon Ott, artistic director of the Seattle Repertory Theatre, describing her production of *A Midsummer Night's Dream* to an interviewer. She argued that approaching Shakespeare with a limiting concept (she gave the example of setting *Taming of the Shrew* in the Wild West) can make clearer the daunting task of forming a strong point of view concerning the multilayered text, but it may not allow for the "elasticity" of mood, emotion, and theme available. *Elasticity* is a great term for Shakespeare's far-reaching applicability. Another commonly used analogy for the interpretation of Shakespeare's ideas is that each play is a prism through which themes are refracted in a variety of colors.

Allowing for the multiplicity of meaning in a Shakespearean play is sometimes antithetical to the presentation of a strong or clarifying personal vision onstage. How to preserve the sensual, emotional, and intellectual subtleties of Shakespeare while creating a production that is theatrically cohesive and relevant to modern experience? I don't count myself among those who believe that Shakespeare isn't Shakespeare without tights and swords. Museum-piece productions may limit a play as severely as misguided updates. One benefit an artist enjoys over others in society is that his works may grant him eternal life. Not so for the playwright whose dramas are trapped with his bones in the historical crypt. The words of Shakespeare, like those of any other playwright, are fated to live or die in the hearts, minds, and hands of every new interpreter, be he historian or avant-garde revisionist.

To breathe fresh life into a play, a director and her cronies must form a personal and imaginative connection with it. They agree upon a shared illusion. Like children creating a make-believe kingdom in the woods, those who stage a play buy into the game 100 percent. The script is their treasure map. The concept is their plan of action. If they are successful, the audience will accept this world and will enter into the illusion. If they fail, the audience will see their creation as a fake, and though parts of the experience may engage their attention, they will be unlikely to make the leap of faith necessary to fully join in the experience.

Coming up with a production concept is ultimately the director's job. His ideas, of course, are subject to modification due to the budget, the producer, or the talents and input of his designers and performers. Many factors may fine-tune a concept. But if the director isn't compelled to follow what he instinctively knows to be important about a play, the production will usually be unbalanced: over designed, unevenly acted, or capriciously theatrical with no deeper impact. The possibilities for going astray are endless. Most productions begin with a meeting in which the director talks to her designers about the play. Depending on the director's style and her preparedness, this meeting may include discussion of a concept, or less specifically, it provides an opportunity for the various production members to fall in love with the play through their director's personal attachment and fascination with the piece.

Recently, I had my first meeting for an upcoming production of

The Grand Magic by Eduardo de Filippo. In my preliminary reading of the play, I had little interest in its characters and situation. Though the piece was rich in costume possibilities, its style was confusing to me. I cynically described de Filippo as a desultory version of Feydeau. But a dose of directorial enthusiasm changed my attitude completely. Mladen Kiselov, a European much more cognizant of the historical and sociological contexts for the play, mesmerized me with his admiration for de Filippo's place in post–World War II Italy. He opened up an unthought-of visual panoply for me — neorealism, early Fellini, surrealism, poetic estrangement. I was thrilled at the prospect of finding parallels between the Italian world of high fashion and the aimless, anesthetized world of post-Fascist nouveau riche society. Mladen's concept was, as yet, embryonic; he knew that he wanted each of the three sets to be built one upon the other, so that the final image would be a kind of triple exposure. In contrast to this expressive background, mirroring the confused psyche of the major character, my costumes were to have a clarifying reality. Class differences were to be strongly defined. The beautiful were to be artfully exquisite and the crass unflinchingly overt. No, the director did not tell me what each character was to wear, but he described a world for me so particular in his imagination that I could see its shadows in my mind. Next I will research Italy, 1946 through 1949 seeking details of personality and style to turn these shadows into concrete forms. I have no doubt that Mladen will recognize the right and wrong images immediately. We have worked together before and forged a bond of trust in taste and discernment. The concept may not be clearly spelled out, but it exists in our joint consciousness of what the play must reveal.

So the concept of each production, whether it be an overt "this for that" revision of the play's period and place or a less ultimately visible clarifying statement of the play's major action and theme, gives the production team a guideline. When the director isn't around, the costume designer, concept in mind, may make logical choices about what will add to the shared illusion.

I once designed a production under the direction of Giles Havergall who, at that time, ran the Citizen's Theatre in Glasgow, Scotland. The play *Figaro!* had been combined from two works by Beaumarchais: *The Barber of Seville* and *The Marriage of Figaro.* Mr. Havergall, who had previously created and directed the play at his own theater, wanted the actors to resemble a bunch of extravagant, gypsy players, pulling from a fanciful trunk of theatrical costumes spanning the entire eighteenth century. Every time I presented a sketch too clearly reminiscent of a recognizable eighteenth-century silhouette, he would ask me to come up with something more raw, startling, or perverse. As I made revisions, I reminded myself over and over that Beaumarchais' plays were thought to be precursors of the French Revolution. The director's intent was not merely to encourage outrageous invention. He wanted me to explode the norms of eighteenth-century style and propriety as the seditiously amusing Beaumarchais sought to expose the depravities and extremes of eighteenth-century class and power. Conscious of this populist imperative, I went about my research slightly differently, rejecting some material that at first seemed perfectly suited to an outlandish style. Specifically, in illustrations from the end of the eighteenth century when fashion excess was epitomized by Frenchmen and women known as "Les Incroyables" and "Les Mervielleuses," I found many examples of apparel taking off on what had recently come before. I realized that mimicking these wealthy extremists might lead me in the right direction, but it would not take me to the right place. Figaro was a servant and the players enacting our production of *Figaro!*

were low-class vagabonds. They might pick up or steal an odd piece of aristocratic finery, but their consciousness was revolutionary and unrefined. Their wardrobe would more likely be influenced by conventions of folk costume than those of courtly pomp and circumstance. What could have been an open-ended designerly free-for-all was held in check and guided by conceptual purpose.

How much can a concept actually be projected onto the actor's body in the form of a costume? Not all that much if the performers aren't to look foolish. The ideal costume is not a sandwich board, bending the shoulders of the poor actor with its all-important message. If a costume impedes the contact made between actor and audience, it does the play a disservice. This applies as much to a costume that tries too hard to illustrate a character's inner life, prohibiting the audience from making their own discoveries through the unfolding story and behavior of the actor. The dark, greasy, mustached villain and the mini-skirted slut are obvious. Equally so is the earnest do-gooder with a "Save the Whales" T-shirt. Why not give him a Denver Broncos T-shirt? Don't worry if the audience doesn't know who he is in his first thirty seconds onstage. It's not necessarily the costume designer's job to tell them.

There are times when a character can't speak for himself; perhaps he is part of the chorus in a musical or opera. In such cases, the costumes may be called upon to "tell it all." The most broadly conceptual costumes I have designed were for an atonal opera by Sir Michael Tippett. The opera *Icebreak* was set in 1960s America. Amid an anonymous chorus representing various factions of civil insurrection and racial violence, the more personal story of the main characters unfolded. I worked with a codesigner, Polly Smith, who opted to design for the nine lead singers, costumed in intensely colored but realistic clothes — realistic, that is, within the norms of 1960s fashion, which gave her quite a bit of scope. I designed the chorus of forty, who, for budgetary reasons, could have only one costume apiece. We decided to keep the chorus in black and white, and I designed a variety of emblematic sixties shapes for them. On the plain white garments, we silk-screened images from black-and-white news photos of the period. As a group, they made a fairly striking background for the solid colors of the lead singers. Looking back, this approach seems heavy-handed, indeed. But then, the opera itself was fairly abstract and propagandistic. In such extended cases where concept may dominate character, my goal is to keep the costumes in some kind of balance with the other production elements (sets, sound, lights) and to enhance the impact of the performers.

Though important to the designers, a concept is frequently indiscernible to the audience. What has been a complexly nuanced puzzle, assembled with obsessive care by the costumer, should, if she is successful, appear to be an effortlessly coordinated whole. Like flower arranging, if the look is too contrived it may be inaccessible, but if it's too haphazard, the design is likely to be uninspiring. Given a choice, I favor too much control over too little, but my designs have run the gamut from highly conceptual to right out of the actor's closet.

On the blatantly contrived end of the scale were a group of costumes for Marivaux's *The Triumph of Love*. In the tradition of commedia dell' arte, many of its characters are variations on famously recognizable clowns including Harlequin, Smeraldina, Brighella, and Pantalone. Their bizarrely ornamented and masked costumes, handed down from Italy to France over the centuries, offer a wealth of extended conventions to draw upon, or to reinvent. What's more, the play has two cross-dressing females, always fun in terms of fashion fantasy and sexual innuendo. The setting, according to the script, is an eighteenth-century formal garden, and John Conklin was the designer. His fantastical site became an amalgam of deconstructed elements: a giant urn, black-and-white photographic blowups of formal gardens, and one delicate green neon tube at the bottom of the surround. One obvious thing missing from this garden was shrubbery or foliage of any kind, which prompted me to conceive the costumes as a kind of moving topiary. Because eighteenth-century clothing silhouettes were artificial and sculptural in the extreme, the leap between contrived bush pruning and contrived apparel making was surprisingly easy to negotiate. Everyone, with the exception of the outsider Harlequin, wore shades of green, some running to blue, some to yellow. The shapes were formal, but my attempt was to make them comical or zany as well. Even the wigs had touches of green, blue, or strawlike yellow. My greatest concern was the reputed fact that green costumes are highly unlucky. "Baste in green, never be seen." Happily, none of my actors were superstitious. What amazed me most about people's reactions to the clothes was that few even mentioned their greenness. In the context of the basically nonchromatic set, the green costumes did make sense. I doubt that anyone actually thought they were bushes, but the shapes of the clothing filled in an imaginary expectation.

Contemporary plays are generally less susceptible to concepts than are lavish period pieces, but not invariably. Beckett, Pirandello, even Pinter, Shephard, and Mamet provide the singular characters and rarified situations that lend themselves to a design concept. A case could be made for subjecting Miller or Williams to a concept. I once designed *A Streetcar Named Desire* for an Eastern European director who told me that Stanley's impact should be like that of a piece of Fascist architecture. His appearance was to proclaim his impassive domination. As an example, the director pointed out a newly erected corporate headquarters, whose magnificence imposed itself on the skyline of the city in which we were working. The building, though much touted among forward-thinking postmodernists, was a scourge to the more nostalgic preservationists in the city. Stanley still ended up in a bowling shirt and work pants, but the image of that building helped me make decisions about how to set Stanley slightly apart from his fellows, and certainly from Blanche.

As a rule, more discussion is devoted to a character's motivation than to his conceptual significance when wardrobing modern plays. I recently designed a production of Neil Simon's *The Odd Couple*. Trying to impress my director, I put forth the theory that Oscar and company were really behaving like Peter Pan and the lost boys. "Yessss," he agreed patiently, and proceeded to the next character detail. Admittedly, this perception had nowhere to go. Was I going to dress them in skins and wooden swords? No, Maury needed a police athletic league jacket and Oscar needed a dirty T-shirt and a baseball cap — end of concept.

My discussion of concepts began with Shakespeare and must return to him, because he gets more than his fair share of brilliant ones. Particularly susceptible are his plays, including the aforementioned *A Midsummer Night's Dream*, that involve two contrasting worlds: the Roman and Egyptian Empires in *Antony and Cleopatra*, Duke Frederick's court and the Forest of Arden in *As You Like It*. One difficulty in costuming such bisected plays is to differentiate between the two locales, while maintaining a unified look for the play as a whole. I have designed *As You Like It* and have seen several good productions of it. Invariably, I have come away unsatisfied by the wildly uneven treatment of the three major sets of costumes — the court, the forest, and the final wedding scene. One group inevitably gets short shrift, usually the court costumes that tend to be approached in an exaggeratedly negative way, emphasizing the evil of

Duke Frederick's court as opposed to the open-handed goodness of Duke Senior and his band in the Forest of Arden. In my time, negative courts have often been translated into Fascist courts where the rulers wear dour, faintly militaristic garb. These costumes inevitably fall into the dead zone. Making autocratic rulers look drab and aesthetically impaired fits back into the category of sandwich-board costume design and is inherently not dynamic. People don't always have to look mean just because they are mean or because their politics are bad. After all, Henry VIII was quite a stylish fellow, not to mention George IV or, in his younger days, Frederick the Great. In *As You Like It*, Rosalind and Celia are "good guys" in the bad court. Should they fit in, since Celia is the Duke's daughter and Rosalind his niece? Or should they look slightly out of place? But the Duke's a despot, so they can't look too unacceptable. Then, how out of place should they look in the forest, where spiritually they belong? Oh to come up with a concept that covers everyone!

Talk is the only salvation. A picture may be worth a thousand words, but in illustrating the complexities of a Shakespearean world, many more than a thousand words are needed before you can begin to draw the pictures. First you talk with the director, the dramaturg, and your fellow designers; then you talk with them again. Often I have left a design meeting, even a lengthy and productive one, thinking that I had the answers and was ready to draw, only to find, as I came to a crucial yet underdiscussed set of characters, that I was unable to figure out where they lived in the world we had imagined. In reconvening with the production team, I discover the set designer has hit a similar wall and the director, in thinking further about the play, has decided our previous ideas were too limiting. Time for further deliberation.

Certainly many concepts would never see the light of day were they scrutinized with a little more thought and discussion. I designed my most nearly traditional English Renaissance costumes for a Shakespearean production on which I had the most numerous and prolonged predesign discussions. This seems particularly ironic since the play in question, *The Tempest*, customarily lends itself to heavy conceptualization. Considered Shakespeare's final play, it is held by many to be an allegory for the theatrical process itself. Prospero's magic gives many designers license to conceive all manner of fantastical and theatrical adornments. In our original concept, the clothes were moving in the direction of timeless, futuristic, postapocalyptic tributes to *Road Warrior*. Caliban was to be the victim of horrendous nuclear bomb burns, and Ariel was a fatigues-and-camouflage-netting kind of battlefield scavenger. What we could never figure out with this approach was: Where the heck did the guys from Sebastian's court come from? Any attempt to put them into a modern or futuristic idiom seemed too anachronistic or too glib for what we found important in the play.

After weeks of discussion with our design team and with our dramaturg Michael Dixon, the director Jon Jory simplified and unified his concept. When all was said and done, he wanted this production of *The Tempest* to center around the cessation of revenge and the regenerative power of forgiveness. By overproducing our concept, we feared that we were wandering too far away from the most significant action of the play.

Our eventual design maintained the sense that Prospero's Island had once been decimated by a human conflict. Whether the place was Troy, Hiroshima, or some sixteenth-century battleground, we tried to obscure. The point was the place was barren. After the initial storm and shipwreck, Sebastian (Prospero's traitorous brother) and his court appeared in tatters, victims of Prospero's furious and vengeful magic. So for the audience's first encounter with the court, they were stripped down, relegated to the universal level of survival. One could understand them as fellow creatures, not posturing Elizabethan players. *The Tempest's* story of brotherly betrayal, revenge, and forgiveness is accessible to modern logic, though its magical incantations and courtly ceremonies may be remote. Reducing the court's elaborate Renaissance costumes to nonspecific rags in the first act, we tried to achieve the humanizing aim of contemporary productions, while keeping within an Elizabethan context, in which many of the external events would seem more plausible. By the time the courtiers reappeared, their sixteenth-century finery restored by means of Prospero's magic staff, they were truly transformed from the ill-defined wreckage of wrath and destruction into the stuff of Shakespearean pageantry.

When Prospero finally doffs his magic robe and resumes the civilized trappings of his former life, the hope was that he and his court would return wiser for their experience on the ruined island. Prospero's forgiveness of Sebastian and of Caliban, his freeing of Ariel, and the betrothal of his daughter Miranda to Ferdinand, the son of his usurping brother, all point to a more peaceful future. At the end of the production, a simple white flower rose through the sand and bloomed on the empty stage.

Was this the definitive production of *The Tempest?* No, but it illustrates the extent to which a concept may change as a director, dramaturg, and design team agree upon their purpose. I do believe that those who saw the production sensed a commitment and unity of vision stemming from long and careful discussion of the play.

Shakespearean plays have always been conceived and produced in modern dress. This applies equally to the seventeenth, eighteenth, nineteenth, twentieth, and twenty-first centuries. In his day,

Shakespeare and company purportedly wore their own clothes to perform his plays — even the history plays, such as *Julius Caesar* set a millennium before the advent of the Elizabethan farthingale and the slashed doublet. In designing updated Shakespearean productions in which the characters wear contemporary clothing, I have had best results working on those plays driven by acts of prejudice, envy, and deception rather than the more fantastical ones. Staging a production of *Othello* with Director Jon Jory and Set Designer Ming Cho Lee, our approach was very different than that in our previous collaboration on *The Tempest*. Ming, who had designed several successful sets for *Othello*, wanted to move away from the accepted image of the Moor storming about in a gorgeous caftan. He argued that the distancing effect of sumptuous period costumes soft-peddled the issues of racism, jealousy, and trust at the core of the tragedy. *Othello*, again, is a play set in two distinct locales: the formal, political world of Venice and the unruly outpost of Cyprus. Strongly opposed to portraying Cyprus in an appealingly exotic or sumptuous light, Jon wished to emphasize the shift in atmosphere from a "civilized" council chamber to an unstable war zone. Othello, a career soldier, inured to the necessities of battlefield law and order, is unpracticed in the workings of political intrigue. He falls prey to the diabolical Iago who convinces him that the mores of subtle Venetians such as Cassio and Desdemona flout the straightforward operations of Othello's passion and honor.

Our 1990s production of *Othello* coincided with several well-publicized incidents in which women had been harassed and maltreated at the hands of their military compatriots or spouses. The question often in the news was whether the testosterone-injected atmosphere of army life made men, in close proximity to women, liable to acts of sexual barbarity. How contemporary *The Tragedy of*

Othello appeared in this light. By mutual agreement, I began to search for a modern idiom in which to costume the play. Ming preferred to set the period back somewhat from our present decade to maintain a balanced perspective and avoid glib topical references. Being unsure about the exact when of our production, I decided to concentrate on the where. Since a majority of the play's action takes place on Cyprus, I began researching its topography, climate, and culture to better understand how people, of Shakespeare's day or my own, would need to dress there. The island has remained a contentious location since Shakespeare's story of Venetian and Turkish conflict. As recently as the 1960s, Cyprus was the scene of warfare between Greeks and Turks, vying for control of the divided island. Studying photographs of this late dispute, I became convinced that the 1960s held the key to costuming our contemporary production of Othello.

Fashion is constantly making references to itself. What is old is new and soon is old again. In the late 1990s, at the time of our *Othello* production, clothing designers were pirating the simple lines of Jackie Kennedy's era. (Think Helen Hunt accepting the 1997 Best Actress Oscar for *As Good As It Gets.* Hadn't you seen photographs of that strapless gown before? Maybe it was a 1960s White House function honoring Andre Malraux — Isaac Stern played a concert after dinner. The only difference was the First Lady was wearing long white gloves.) In picking a modern period other than the present, it's always more appealing to reference a look that is in rather than one that presently seems dated and hopelessly misguided. In other words, 1980s padded shoulders and big hair would inappropriately distract an audience newly attuned to 1990s minimalism, even if a political reference to that decade made sense. Setting up a reverberation between the tastes and norms of our own time, a time recently past, and a time long past is particularly interesting for a theatrical costume designer. By drawing from the minimal and elegant shapes of 1960s couture, I tried to create a "classic" modern look for Desdemona and Emilia. For the military men, I immersed myself in the surprisingly diverse and painterly world of camouflage. I learned that the Greek, Turkish, and Cypriot forces in the 1960s were supplied with arms and uniforms from other countries, France and Russia among them. Since camouflage, though specific to terrain and climate, has an indefinite post–World War I look, I was able to give the soldiers a modern-day combat appearance without referring to an easily recognizable military campaign. At the time, Desert Storm camouflage was easily available but would make a completely inappropriate reference. I ended up buying a variety of woodland camouflage from a former mercenary soldier with international connections — don't ask, don't tell. For the Venetians, I looked at 1960s photographs of Italian and Greek politicians and power figures. Not surprisingly, the dark suits and horn-rimmed glasses worn by statesmen in almost every photograph were interchangeable with those favored by their counterparts thirty years later. Working closely with the director and set designer to coordinate the use of weapons, physical fights, architectural elements, and furniture choices, we sought to contemporize *Othello*'s inevitably violent intersection of war, race, and sex.

Whether mounting a production of *Othello*, *King Lear*, or *The Three Penny Opera*, a production concept enables a designer to build an imaginary scaffolding from which she may view the play at every angle and approach it on a firm footing. Plays, particularly the large and famous ones, are daunting to a designer who must examine every inch of every character, one by one, scene after scene. Any plan that will allow the many visual questions to be addressed in some systematic and holistic way prevents the various participants from falling back on divergent personal tastes. Instinct may be the fundamental mechanism of any designer, but left unchecked, without purpose, it can go astray. I have rarely known a costume designer who could not find something to love in a period or culture. There is no such thing as an ugly color. Chance visual encounters can sway my imagination at the drop of a hat. An exhibit of Amish quilts, a Pierre Bonnard retrospective, a closeout sale at Thai Silks, a flowering hydrangea bush can literally saturate my consciousness. The production concept helps put blinders on an all too promiscuous sensibility. If I have good reason to be committed to a monochromatic production of *A Doll's House*, I won't be tempted by an errant infatuation with color to veer toward fabrics perfectly suitable to another production but wrong for this austere one.

I remember coming to the end of my four years as a college English major, utterly exhausted with the process of writing papers proposing fresh slants on major literary works. "Neo Platonism in Blake's 'The Book of Thel'" comes to mind. By comparison, costume design seemed so practical and concrete. In fact, as a costume designer, I continue the same process of reaction and analysis, now using paint and fabric rather than written words to express my point of view. Every production design is really a visual essay. With my director and fellow designers, I build a case for my interpretation of a play and present that interpretation for the audience to accept or reject. The production concept guides our collective efforts to rekindle the life force of a play and to reveal it in fresh and vital form.

As I prepare for my upcoming opportunity to see *A Midsummer Night's Dream*, *Cymbeline*, and *Hamlet* in rapid succession, I relish the enlarging experience of understanding each of the plays through the minds of three exceptional directors. Whether I will go along with them or separate myself somewhere in act 2, I am secure in the hard-won knowledge that Shakespeare has the stuff to survive almost any concept.

Chapter Seven

New Plays

DESIGN IMPROVISATION

In 1983, I took a job as resident costume designer at the Actors Theatre of Louisville (ATL). The previous spring, a *New York Times* review of Jane Martin's *Talking With* called my attention to ATL's annual New Play Festival. Designing new work appealed to me, and here was a place committed to the task. So, I moved to Kentucky. During my first season there, I costumed thirty-two new plays (albeit twenty-one were one-acts). Within the space of seven months, I worked with Emily Mann, Jane Martin, John Pielmier, Horton Foote, and Romulus Linney. I got hooked. What began as a one- or two-year commitment to a low-paying but novel learning experience became a sixteen-year odyssey.

Why do I love new plays? Because they're so "out there." Playwrights have little to gain and plenty to lose, but you name it, they take it on. They tell our secrets. They do it naked, they do it in uniforms, they do it in cothurni (high-platform footwear used in ancient Greek and Roman drama), they do it disguised as yetis, they do it looking just like the guy next door. Unlike politicians in the business of assuring us that everything is under control, playwrights disturb us by invoking the disorder beneath life's surface. You might cross the street to avoid any number of their characters. But in the anonymity of your theater seat, you'll listen to them. Hearing their secrets, you flush with recognition or bristle with annoyance. You have a window on the world outside your comfort zone, and you peer through the blinds.

New plays, which generally deal with contemporary life, push costume designers into edgy territory. Outfitting a production in the Byzantine or even the late Victorian period, I have research and can stand as the authority on what people should wear. Costuming modern dress, everyone's an expert, and anyone might have an opinion worth considering. Consequently, my work on contemporary productions becomes rather improvisational.

In our media-rich daily life, researching modern dress would seem to be a snap, but fashion magazines and retail catalogues, in which pictures of up-to-date apparel are easily available, seldom present images that are honest and "alive." My husband, a director, is endlessly frustrated when costume designers show up with catalogues for research. He is disheartened when a character is reduced to a Brooks Brothers type. Catalogues cater to the average person's aspiration to be outwardly identified with some acceptable or desirable norm. Marketers profitably promote the concept that packaging is 70 percent of the battle to belong. Homogenized retail models are basically striped of idiosyncrasy and nuance. High-end fashion magazines, though they strive to set trends rather than cater to them, present icons more startling, but similarly devoid of character.

Plays only rarely deal with the beautiful people. If they do, these paragons are seldom at their best. The characters I most enjoy costuming are *not* measuring up to what is deemed beautiful or appropriate. As I look around me, it appears that real life defies style. In similar ways, theater often subverts the act of "arriving." Characters are introduced at the intersection of expectation and disappointment. They're busy becoming or disintegrating, and giving them a trite or polished look is deadening.

What people really wear, in my opinion, is more fascinating than what they wish they could wear. For instance, what would the woman sitting at her computer ordering from the Victoria's Secret catalogue be wearing? By the end of the day, does the normal fly fisherman bear any resemblance to his buff counterparts from the pages of L.L. Bean? Nine to one, a commuter on a crowded bus or subway reading the latest fashion periodical has a myriad of quirks, perhaps more pragmatic, but no less interesting than the supermodels she admires. The details that make an interesting contemporary costume are details that shape and express life, imperfect though it may be. Treading a fine line between noncommittal or boring clothes versus those that are overly contrived or artificially glamorized is what costuming modern dress is about.

I try to look for images not created by a stylist. Borrowing from fashion, advertising, movies, and television is basically secondhand design. News photography provides a more character-based resource. But if photographic coverage of certain odd pockets of humanity is scarce, I seek out the source. Costuming Jane Martin's *Keely and Du*, I was uncertain about how Keely would dress on the day of her abortion. So I called a local clinic. A nurse told me that all prospective clients were advised to wear something loose, comfortable, and easy to get off and on, like sweats. I parked outside the clinic at 7 A.M., took notes and made sketches. To see what Keely's antagonists might look like, I went to a service at the local fundamentalist Christian Church. From direct observation, I learned that a good number of the moral majority appear to shop at JC Penney. I brought my sketches and notes to the next design conference. Though thumbnail sketches and verbal descriptions are more impressionistic than actual photographs, they almost always provoke excellent preliminary discussions with directors. The designer as investigative reporter? Yes.

Just as a costumer of modern dress may give a character a one-dimensional appearance by collecting secondhand, stereotypical research, a director may err by launching into an item-by-item description of the character's clothing before discussing what the character is like. Costume designers always depend on directors to expand their sense of a character's motivations, fears, strengths, and preconceptions and to give each character a function in the play as a whole. Even for a contemporary play, discussion of each character's general psychological and sociological background is crucial. If a costume designer doesn't have a reason for picking every item of clothing, she may literally be adrift in the shopping mall, grabbing whatever item hits her fancy.

One production in which I wrongly re-created a director's "exact" description of how a character should dress stands out in my mind because it was the first time I worked with my future husband, Jon Jory. In our preliminary design discussion, he told me that the young wife in our play should wear a navy-blue skirt and white blouse. The actress cast in the part was bright, outspoken, healthy, athletic, and incredibly beautiful. She should have been easy to costume, but with no more information than the navy skirt and white blouse, my efforts to make her look like the character were dismal. Months later, in a postmortem discussion with Jon and the playwright, I questioned Jon's insistence on the blue skirt and white blouse. "Yeah," chimed in the playwright, "why the Catholic schoolgirl look?" Jon was surprised. "I didn't want her to look like a Catholic schoolgirl. The character you wrote seemed a lot like your wife and I remember one day, she walked into the theater straight from your farm and how wonderful she looked. I think she was wearing a blue skirt and a white blouse." This statement opened up such a different series of ideas for me. If only I had heard it before costuming the play! Not knowing me very well, Jon was unsure about my taste and abilities and thought that getting too specific about the playwright's wife was inappropriate. So, he described what she looked like one day rather than talk about her personality. In truth, the woman to whom he was referring was a unique combination of artist, outdoorswoman, hippie, and savvy careerist. The boring denim skirt and nondescript white blouse I had given the character were about as far from appropriate as could be imagined. Since they weren't actively objectionable, nobody complained, but nobody found the costume very interesting or helpful either. From that point on, I have always tried to get to what is behind a director's advice — more so if the advice is very specific.

Detail discussions often begin too quickly on a new play because conceptual discussions are rare. The presence of a living, breathing playwright may inhibit a director from marking a production with his stamp. Since everyone producing a new play, including the playwright, is often feeling his way through the work, assessing its moment-to-moment playability, the larger picture is not always clear. No one is striving to come up with a new or alternative slant. The object, in the best of situations, is to present the work cleanly and coherently.

Without a concept, directors often rely on their own memories and acquaintances when discussing characters. "This guy is just like my uncle Fred who always wore white socks and black dress shoes, so that's what the actor should wear." Indeed, white socks and black shoes might be just the thing, but functionally, a costume designer gets in trouble if she becomes a shopper rather than an informed decision-maker. What if the actor had a teacher in school who wore white socks and dress shoes but was nothing like the character in question? I am not kidding — just such situations happen all the time in fitting rooms. Actors can be completely put off if personal experience leads them to believe that their clothes are at odds with the characters they're struggling to create. If the costume designer has nothing more to say than, "The director told me that's what you should wear," she will lose credibility. What's worse, she will be uncertain of her alternatives.

Right at the beginning, the costume designer should have questioned the director further. "Tell me more about your uncle Fred. What was he like? Where did he live? How was he educated? Did he care about his clothes or was he clueless? What was his problem with black socks?" As the costumer forms a sense of the real Uncle Fred, she and the director may embark on fruitful discussions about his dramatic counterpart. Later in the fitting room, the costume designer will have a much better time when the actor makes his objection. "You see, this character is wearing the white socks because, as is obvious in the script, he's an obsessive compulsive, and the director and I made up this story that he once read an article about Calvin Coolidge's son who played tennis in black socks, got a blister, and died from blood poisoning when the black dye got into his system. From that day on, the character has always worn white socks, no matter what the situation." The actor, who is probably thrilled to talk with anyone who cares so much about the minutiae of his character, will most likely say something to the effect of, "cool," and that will be the end of the distracting discussion about his high school English teacher.

New plays require great patience, curiosity, and finesse from the costume designer. There are times when a director may feel pressured by preliminary design meetings, wishing to defer decisions until rehearsal when he discovers what the actor will bring to his role. For a costume designer, this may be a wonderful opportunity to cooperate in the creation of a believable, fully formed character. Alternately, it will become a nightmare of indecision, metastasizing into a taste war. The outcome will depend on the assurance and purpose of the director and the security and flexibility of the actor. It also will depend on the costume designer's resilience.

Many times, while designing two or three productions in the Humana Festival of New American Plays, I have worked simultaneously in the shop with other costume designers. Since many actors are double cast, working on two or three plays in rep, information travels quickly between fittings. I have watched productions disintegrate, costume wise, into a battle of wills between the performers and the costume designer. Sadly, the person who usually loses is the actor who ends up onstage in a watered-down version of his original costume, chosen as a compromise, but doing little to define or enhance his character. In such cases, the costume designer usually faults the director, who goes into rehearsal uncertain of who his characters really are. In early design meetings, the director may be compelled by the designer's ideas and give the impression of a go-ahead. Once rehearsals get underway, new acting imperatives take precedence and the interpretation of a role can easily evolve from that which the director and costumer originally discussed. A performer may arrive at her first fitting and state flat out that the costume is totally at odds with her interpretation, impractical for the movement she's required to perform, or just plain ugly and unflattering.

Before I pursue this scenario to its fractious end, let me say that the costume designer has little to gain by pitting himself against a performer. Actors who are really secure about their process seldom become fixated on their costumes. When a performer says that she feels ugly in a costume, at least three things could be wrong. One, the costume may really be ugly and unflattering. Two, the costume may not be ugly and unflattering, but the performer is not seeing what everyone else sees. (When dealing with contemporary clothing, a costume designer is, more than ever, at the mercy of the actor's tastes and preconceptions. Her mother told her she looked fat in kilts and that's all she's ever going to see.) Three, the actor is at a point in the rehearsal process where she's lost. She hasn't really found the character. The director hasn't paid much attention to her because he's more worried about the fact that the play doesn't have an ending. The playwright may have just arrived in town and cut her favorite speech at the end of act 1. In any case, the costume is undoubtedly the tip of the iceberg. Why is it that in so many of these situations, costume designers dig in their heels rather than explore the subtext?

No costume designer wants an actor to look bad, but like the actor, she probably has a hidden agenda. Maybe this kilt, detested by the actress, is the designer's pet shopping coup. It was exactly like her sketch, it was on sale, she bought it (though it was nonreturnable and a little too expensive — even on sale). If only the actress could be made to see reason! What's the typical next step? Go to the director. Usually the actor gets there first and the story is likely to be, "I can't move in this kilt." "I feel totally wrong in this kilt." "It's nothing like what we discussed yesterday about the character being a tomboy." "I can't possibly make my costume change between scenes 1 and 2 if I have to deal with this kilt," and so on. Next, the director gets the costume designer's tale of woe. "Remember in our first discussion when you loved the idea of that kilt, and I found one exactly like the picture? I've already spent 75 percent of my budget for her character on this one kilt because it's so perfect. Would you just come to the next fitting and take a look at it?"

Here's where the director hates to be: in a no-win situation. Any decent director will, of course, choose what's right for the production. In truth, the outcome depends on how well the rehearsal process is going and what kind of time the director is having with the performer in question. I have experienced a number of these fitting-room showdowns, and in hindsight, I must say that the director has seldom been wrong. At this point, both director and actor are closer to the central nervous system of the play. If the actor is truly miserable in her costume, her performance will be none the better for it. What makes these situations really sorry is when the director agrees with the actor, and the costume designer can't or won't come up with a good alternative to her original design. I have seen designers effectively "sign off" from a production, usually characterizing the director as an inconsistent wimp. The designer may go through the paces of getting the clothes together, but the performers and the costume shop all know she disapproves and the play bears her curse.

Here are the ways I think it could go better. First of all, the costume designer only has the right to make decisions on an equal footing with the director and the performers if he has attended a good number of rehearsals. If a designer is in on the day-to-day process of creating a production, he will be more cognizant of what the actor can or cannot wear and what the character should or should not wear. He can make creative contributions within the context of this particular production rather than some idealized production in his head. Plus, his credibility will be about 500 percent higher. Time pressures make such full-out participation difficult, so a designer must be aware that in creating a new work, what seemed like a good idea two weeks before the play was cast may be outdated by the second week of rehearsal. Don't buy anything you can't return.

Rarely does a serious taste war occur in a production where the designer has done honest-to-goodness sketches. Because nobody really knows what's out there in the thrift stores and the shopping malls, designers of modern-dress productions often hedge their bets by showing directors and actors a kind of research storyboard. Instead of really designing a costume, they present a montage of pictures (from catalogues and magazines) and notes to give impressions of what they hope to find. While saving the designer from making promises she can't keep, these paste-ups display so many choices that everyone is likely to come away with a different idea of what the final costume will be. When the real-life, affordable clothing item appears, it usually falls short of somebody's expectations.

Right or wrong, I have much better luck jumping in and making a specific colored sketch rather than showing the actors or the shop a lot of maybes. In sketching, hopefully on an appropriate body type, I can see ahead of time what combinations of jacket, sweater, shorts, or whatever will work together. In the first design presentation, a director is much more likely to be decisive if he's given a clear choice rather than a bunch of possibilities to which he may have varying reactions. Actors, too, may contribute much more positively if they see one distinct image. Right away, the actress could see the kilt and have an opportunity to voice her misgivings. If nothing else, the sketch provides something to argue about. Without it, everyone just assumes the right choices will be made. That assumption is as absurd as traveling with a group of twenty and assuming that if you split off individually, without prearranging any set time or place to meet, everyone will end up at the same restaurant for dinner. A clear costume sketch is an essential starting point whether it ends up bearing any resemblance to the final costume or not.

In dealing with new plays, designers, directors, and actors have similarly conflicting emotions about taking a stand. Almost everyone who works on new plays loves the opportunity to contribute insights. Characters and ideas are fresh, and the first production of a play is almost like a birthing process. All participants feel excitement and tremendous creative energy, at least at the start of the process and hopefully through to the opening night. This intense involvement can make actors and designers more than ordinarily testy when conflicts of perception occur. There's a feeling of parental protectiveness about every idea, which if attached to too much ego and defensiveness can deplete a production tremendously. In counterpoint to this personal connection is the fear of being wrong. "What if I'm the one to screw up this play?" "What if the director doesn't agree with me?" "What if the playwright is horrified?" Such misgivings occur in any production, but they are particularly pronounced in new, untested ones. All the more reason for the costume designer to plunge in there and make a sketch, even a premature one. Somebody's got to be brave enough to be wrong, and the lucky costume designer has the least to lose: He doesn't have to wear the clothes, and he can always blame the director for allowing him to take the

wrong path. His protective coloration allows him to be a provocative instigator, if he is bent on the good of the play rather than the
glory of being right.

When I said that the director is usually right when deciding
between actor and costume designer, I speak of a director mature
enough to handle her own and others' emotions with some perspective. One situation comes to mind that involved a real-life kilt,
the one heretofore described being fictitious. The play in question
centered on a group of high school students who, for the majority
of time, were to appear in school uniforms. The director and costume designer had expended some effort pouring through uniform
catalogues until they agreed upon every element of the student's
school clothing. Their choices had to be made before the actors
began rehearsal, since quantities of such apparel, ordered in the middle of the school year, need time to arrive.

Unfortunately, the lead actress, who had to play a vixenish type,
left her first fitting displeased. She immediately told the director that
her uniform made her feel ugly, claiming that she would be unable
to *act* sexy if she *looked* like a nerd. The director, as evidenced by his
behavior toward the actress, was particularly concerned with her
ability to attract and promised he'd come to the next fitting. There,
at the actress's suggestion, he agreed that the uniform skirt must be
hemmed seven or eight inches above her knees to give the performer what she needed, internally, to carry out her role.

The rest of the cast, being young and also concerned with their
appeal, took the first actress's lead and began to second-guess the costume designer about their uniforms as well as their out-of-school
clothes — the brand names of their sneakers, the cut of their jeans,
and so on. In almost every case, the director, who sat in on all the
fittings, insisted that the actors prevail. The production quickly

began to drain the costume shop's resources; design assistants were sent on countless trips, buying and returning rejected items. Soon the designer was way over budget. The actors' rebellious attitudes snowballed, and by the end of technical rehearsals, they had alienated their dressers with rude behavior and surly demands, exhausted their stage manager, and showed little respect for their director. Not surprisingly, the play was poorly received, lacking coherent objective and tone. The costume designer was so disgusted that she left town without even seeing the first preview.

Hindsight, as usual, is so very easy. In truth, this director's tactic of letting his young actors get into their roles as malicious, destructive teenagers by some kind of method approach in which their every self-serving instinct was to be indulged, probably doomed any clearheaded perspective. But the costume designer was also young and very hip. Her sketches and choices were much more interesting than were those of the actors. Why didn't anyone listen to her? Because she was so insulted that she shut down after minimal attempts to reason with them. She never stooped to cajoling, which at times is more necessary than reasoning. The production really was the worse for losing her taste and talent.

So, in the interest of the play, here's what I think she should have said in that first kilt fitting. "Any school that requires a uniform has a rigorous code about skirt length, i.e., it has to touch the floor when the student is kneeling." (This I think she did say to them, but to no avail.) "Anyone who's ever been outside a parochial school at three o'clock knows that just about every girl rolls her skirt up to her crotch the second she gets out the door. Couldn't the actress hike up her skirt at appropriate points in the play? More important, why make obvious the implicit eroticism of the innocent schoolgirl or boy? The fact that nubile bodies and throbbing hearts beat beneath their innocuous tartans, is one of those tantalizing incongruities of sexual fantasy. If the vixen's sexuality is only suggested in her uniform, what a striking contrast her 'street clothes' will make. Surprise is tremendously seductive."

Whether or not these arguments would have turned the costume designer into a conspirator instead of an adversary, I do not know. I do know that the poor play could certainly have used her goodwill rather than her enmity.

It's very hard for a costume designer to guess when to give in to a difference in taste and when to hold his ground. Trying to maintain a balanced attitude, in which the best instincts of the actor and director are remembered and any ego-dousing slights are discounted, comes with experience or with the luck of having an iron-clad sense of self. When I spot an actor who has the potential to become an opponent, I try to enlist her support by taking her with me to selected stores. This is a luxury that time and budget do not always afford, but like any luxury, it makes life a lot more pleasant. The performer becomes more attuned to budgetary concerns and, as all of us do when we go shopping, confronts the necessity for compromise. The designer, in turn, becomes better acquainted with the actor's body type and can usually draw a pretty accurate bead on what's making her resistant or insecure.

I have rarely had a bad experience shopping with an actor. Once, however, I almost gave up too soon with an older performer who wore clothes extremely well and was taciturn and strongly opinionated. We returned from thrift shopping with a number of selections to show the director. I had a favorite suit that was definitely low on the actor's list and was consistently pushed to the back of the rack when the director arrived in the fitting room. Finally, when we'd spent forty minutes putting on and taking off about six different outfits, the director, Tazwell Thompson, who had been most solicitous about the actor's opinions, graciously turned to me and asked, "Which one do you like best?" Though actor and director seemed well satisfied with several of the existing choices, I, who usually like to simplify rather than complicate, was beguiled by his respectful treatment of my opinion into telling the truth. "Actually, the one I like best is here at the end of the rack, but it may be too formal." "Well, let's see it," said Tazwell. His reaction to the suit was immediate. It was perfect, and his enthusiasm was so genuine that the actor was swayed. So I've learned never to be so eager to keep the peace in a production that I silence my better judgment. The trick is to keep opinions from becoming polarized to the point that recapitulation is unbearable. Stonewall Jackson would not have made a good costume designer. On the other hand, Henry Clay would probably not have made a great director. So much of the success of a new work is dependent not on the director's ability to compromise, but on his capacity to be decisive. Actors and designers alike hate to waste needless time and energy on second-guessing and disagreement. They rely on their director to maintain respect for everyone's contribution and to channel divergent talents in the right direction. The more trust there is in the director, the more harmony there is in the production process — especially when the play is new and success is very uncertain.

Probably more uninteresting than a production in which the costume designer has worked too hard to accommodate the performers is a production that has been too tightly regimented by a designer's "refined" point of view. I recently read a review of a contemporary movie filmed in New York City that marveled how the film had so sanitized the city that it appeared to be a boring place to live. Designers at work! The biggest challenge in modern dress is to balance unity of vision with variety of character. A designer, no matter how avid a people-watcher she may be, has only seen so much, and that through her own discerning filter.

My best costumes have been those in which I have been most in touch with the performers and the director. I would be very dishonest if I were to give the impression that the majority of what goes on between actors and costume designers is conflictual. In most cases, the situation is: the more ideas, the more enjoyable the process, the more interesting the costumes.

Given a good director and an interesting new script, most performers are game to try the outrageous or unexpected. Such an actor is Kathy Bates, whom I costumed in a dark, two-person play, *Two Masters* by Frank Manly. A man and woman, an eerily "simple" backward pair, sat facing the audience on a dilapidated couch for the entire piece. It was Kathy's idea to make her immobile character enormously large, but to try to be absolutely believable in doing so. We worked and worked with layer upon layer of thin quilting, creating bulbous limbs and pendulous waddles filled with split peas. She pulled her hair in a flat black net and with subtle, subversive makeup was able to make herself look thirty years older and congenitally unhealthy. The real brilliance of this event came from the frightening deadness she created within. But I took what reflected glory I could from a costume far more troubling and theatrical than I would ever have assembled without tapping into Kathy's intuition and daring.

Lesser versions of the same situation happen all the time. I'm embarrassed to admit that I habitually depend on actors to steer me away from my tendency to match everything. I once heard a costume design intern being mocked because she refused to go out jogging unless her running shoes matched her sweats. My uncomprehending reaction was, "Of course not!" The intern and I understood each other completely. Yes, costume designers can get carried away. On occasion, somebody has to jolt them into the world of other, less color-coordinated mortals. Not everyone has the time or inclination to assemble the perfect outfit. I recently costumed a new play by Jane Martin in which one of the characters was a Hollywood starlet. I was so busy scouring the pages of *Vanity Fair* and *W* to find the coolest, most stunning looks for her, I neglected to consider that some of the scenes took place in nonpublic places like a hotel room or a gym. I found an exquisite Thai sarong for the character to wear for a late-night scene where she was drinking with other females in her bedroom. Determined to find the ideal sexy top to go with the sarong, I subjected the young actress Caitlin Miller to a long process of elimination. Finally, Caitlin, who had worked with me before, appealed for a reprieve from design. "What about if I just throw on a big old white shirt with this and tie it at the waist?" Of course, she looked great — far more comfortable and in fact sexier than in some other scenes where she wore tight, plunging, starlet tops. Designing, which involves selecting and refining, is often at odds with character building, which involves combining and pragmatizing. Actors and costume designers, particularly in contemporary work, need one another to build a look that is sharp and surprising and, at the same time, true.

The most unique and incomparably interesting opportunity afforded by new plays is the chance to work with playwrights. I am aware that others do not share this opinion. I once spoke on a panel concerned with designing new theatrical work. I was the only costume designer, sitting with three set designers and a lighting designer. About two-thirds of the way through the event, I began to feel that I might have been working all these years in another universe from my design colleagues. The question came up, "How much do you actually work with the playwright in creating your designs?" To a man, and it was true that for some strange reason I was the only woman on the panel, the set and lighting designers agreed that getting too involved with playwrights was very risky. The reasoning seemed to be that playwrights thought they knew, but didn't really know, what they wanted. What a playwright deemed necessary to the environment of his work was often shortsighted and overly literal. Worse yet was direct involvement with a playwright who dealt in abstractions. The result was often an unworkable scenic nightmare. No, my fellow designers felt that any substantive communication between playwrights and designers should take place through the director. Realizing that I had been uncharacteristically quiet during this discussion, the moderator asked if I was in agreement. "Well, no," I had to answer honestly, since I could recognize no part of my experience in the previous opinions. "I love to talk with playwrights, and I don't believe that I've ever worked with a director who didn't encourage me to do so." Debate ensued, and I felt hopelessly corny and idealistic by the end. Later, I was pulled aside by several playwrights and directors who thanked me for voicing my point of view.

My only explanation for the incongruity between my methods and those of my fellow set and lighting designers (whom I greatly admire and respect) harkens back to the hierarchy of theater. Set and lighting designers work in more hallowed and definitely less populated territory. Costume designers, directly involved with actors, are accustomed to handling suggestions unfiltered by directorial approval. Costuming involves a great deal of arcane personal minutiae unlikely to be on the top of a director's priority list. If a playwright is interested in talking to me about clothes and character, most directors are delighted to receive this information gleaned from an

alternative perspective. Maybe playwrights know more about people, and therefore what people wear, than they do about space and
light. In any case, I have never been given a false lead by a playwright, nor have I been offered costume ideas that were ultimately
impossible or improbable. Only in the realm of idealized or archetypical beauty (the ingenue in white) have I gotten into unnaviga-
ble waters. To be fair, playwrights are not alone in having an
inchoate idea of male or female perfection to which assigning an ordinary physical form is very, very difficult. Rarely will a playwright
be the single one responsible for derailing the process of agreement.
The challenge is to come up with one form mutually acceptable to
director, playwright, actor, and designer.

I can recall countless preliminary phone conversations with
playwrights in which I've been privy to invaluable clothing subtext.
"Why have I written that she should wear a red sweater? Well I think
my sister has had this one red sweater since high school, and I remember the night our mother died she had it on, and it seemed so
strange to me. There she was with gray hair and tired eyes and her
sweater was the same. She'll probably be wearing it when she's
eighty; I guess she's just herself in it. I think it's red, or maybe you'd
call it cranberry . . . " So, from reading the succinct stage direction
(*She wears a red sweater*), I might have mistakenly gone out and
bought a brand-new, bright red sweater, not understanding that the
character was dressing for comfort rather than show — not a major
point, but enough to lead me in the wrong direction.

Having had the pleasure of talking with and picking the brains
of so many playwrights, I now feel really bereft when designing plays
without one. My experiences have run the gamut from playwrights
who involve themselves in every decision to more reticent ones who
contribute enigmatic, evocative clues rather than outright opinions.

I worked in the former manner with Naomi Itzuka, designing her play *Polaroid Stories*. At first, I was hesitant to take on the project, worried that I was too old to effectively design costumes for homeless teenagers. Michael Dixon, the production dramaturg, suggested that I call Naomi and get her opinion. Before doing so, I talked with the director who was interested in my designing the piece, understood my limitations, and agreed that Naomi was the person who knew most about these characters and could give me the best sense about whether I could understand them. *Polaroid Stories,* I think it is fair to say, is a play difficult to fully conceive from a first reading. Not having heard the play read aloud, I was initially handicapped in my ability to flesh out the characters.

Speaking with Naomi had a profound impact on me. She was so viscerally acquainted with each of her characters, yet did not consider any one to be a closed book. She talked of them as a sister might talk of a beloved, but slightly feared, schizo-phrenic brother. Naomi helped me understand the individual egos of these tormented individuals. She suggested what their clothing might do to define them, comfort them, or hide them. Without calling into question my lack of knowledge on this subject, she gave me specific descriptions of kids she had observed or met and recommended several books of photographs. Adding another layer, Naomi described the figures from Greek mythology with whom her modern characters were poetically connected.

As she constructed this bridge between the highly specific street kids and their mythological counterparts, I began to see how I could assist the production. The key, really, was not how perfectly I could re-create the look of modern-day teenage runaways nor the classic appearance of legendary Greek characters, but how I might invoke a creative suggestion of the latter in the metaphorical depiction of the former. In other words, my knowledge of archaic Greek clothing could assist the poetic process of theatricalizing your basic grungy street punks.

I eventually conferred with Naomi on almost every trivial detail. The process involved a lot of trial and error. Since the director was very open to our collaboration, he encouraged me to send actors up to rehearsal in various versions of their costumes. (We weren't worried about rips or stains, since the characters were supposedly living in their clothes.) In so doing, Naomi, the actors, and the director could see how the costumes worked with the developing characterizations. Sometimes I would be pushing too far into the abstract, iconographic world, and sometimes the clothes would look too prosaic and familiar. The fine-tuning was a detailed process of adding and subtracting small elements. In the end, I was extremely proud of the costumes, and well aware that I could never have created them alone.

There have been other situations in which I was not so completely dependent on the playwright's involvement but was nonetheless inspired by it. By definition, a good writer has powers of communication more highly developed than most of us. Though every playwright is not necessarily voluble, once launched on a discussion of a character or image close to her heart, she is apt to be vividly descriptive. A particular incident involving Romulus Linney may illustrate.

I was designing the costumes for a one-act version of *Love Suicides at Schofield Barracks*. In a phone conversation, Romulus told me about two Noh masks that were part of the production. I had to make the masks, and I was questioning him about which of the many traditional Noh faces might be appropriate. Since this was our first conversation and we didn't have pictures to look at, he described for me two masks he had purchased in Japan, which had been the catalysts for the climactic scene in *Loves Suicides*.

Though he was not concerned that I produce masks exactly like his, we were amazed when he arrived on the scene, late in the rehearsal process, to discover that one of the masks I had chosen to copy was identical to his, and the other uncannily similar. The shades of expression, which distinguish many traditional Noh masks from one another, are often very subtle. It was hardly coincidental that the masks I chose from dozens of others in my research were so close to those that had inspired this play. Romulus's description of each mask's emotional impact had been brief but conveyed the salient theatrical gestures so well I could recognize their pictures.

Some playwrights really don't want to explain themselves. My only preproduction conversation with Charles Mee took place at the first rehearsal of his play *Big Love* when it was produced at ATL's Twenty-fourth Humana Festival. He had managed to evade my early phone calls, so I was nervous about presenting my sketches at the "show and tell" without having ever talked to him. When asked to say a few words about the play, he basically praised the director, Les Waters, was extremely grateful that so excellent a cast had been assembled, and reacted with unfeigned enthusiasm to the set model and costume sketches. What he had to say was written. What we would say was yet to come. He hoped we would enjoy ourselves, and he looked forward to seeing our work. So saying, he left the city and stayed away until first preview, which, I'm glad to report, was a popular and critical success. On a practical level, I had no real interaction with Charles. But spiritually, his openness and trust were extremely compelling. All of us were that much more committed to

Les because of the playwright's obvious belief in him, and we were inspired to delight Charles when he returned to see what we would add to his wildly imaginative piece.

Working on new plays is, perhaps, so engaging because they involve a particular intimacy and innocent hopefulness. It's an exploratory rather than a final process. A second marriage is sometimes a sounder, saner marriage, but the charms and calamities of a first marriage have their own indisputable value. So it happens that later productions may have bigger budgets, bigger stars, and greater glory, yet they are built on the backs of a play's early productions. One thing unanimously agreed upon in the aforementioned colloquia on designing new work was that none of the designers present enjoyed redesigning or remounting productions of a successful new play.

Though I have been asked on a number of occasions to follow a production Off Broadway or to another regional theater, I have only agreed to do so twice, once very disastrously and once successfully. The successful production was the early John Patrick Shanley play *Danny and the Deep Blue Sea*, starring John Turturro and June Stein. A two-character work involving only about four costumes, *Danny* was so simple in its conception and so clearly focused on the compelling work of the actors, all I had to do was keep out of its way. I ended up shipping the original costumes to New York and had little involvement with its ensuing success.

The disastrous remount I won't detail but it had the hallmarks of many second productions: complacent, overdefined, overacted, overdesigned. What I had to contribute, I contributed much more freely and daringly in the first production. Redesigning the clothes, I just overstated the obvious. Basically, remounting a production is not as much fun. In my experience, when theatrical artists aren't enjoying themselves it shows. Better to let a new designer come on the scene with new things to learn, new things to contribute, and new things to prove. For years I was mildly ashamed about this attitude. When I heard several other designers voicing their dislike and avoidance of second productions, I was tremendously relieved.

The limited income and uncertain reception that are part and parcel of producing new plays do not attract every designer. Disappointment comes in greater measure than success. Many of my favorite plays never make the cut. They aren't marketable: They won't attract a broad audience, they won't serve as a star vehicle, they won't function as a diverting perk in an evening of business entertainment. I am hopelessly attracted to work from the heart: plays that offer poetic or imagistic truths. Often defying a "real-life" format, they land on an über-real-life psychological or philosophical plane that I find breathtaking. For those of us who root for the underdog or enjoy the inevitability of uncertainty and change, the opportunity to collaborate on an early production delivers unequaled rewards.

Chapter Eight

Success and Failure

LEARNING FROM BOTH

Badly designed costumes, unlike badly designed buildings, have a relatively short life span and will eventually disappear from view. More than any other question I am asked, "What do you do with the costumes after a play is over?" I answer this question evasively, because rarely am I completely satisfied with my work, and by the final performance, even the costumes I did like are so tired that they bear little resemblance to my original flawless conceptions. "Sometimes theaters rent them or reuse them," I answer, trying not to sound wasteful. "But I don't have much to do with the costumes once a play opens. By then, I'm hopefully onto the next project." Each play gives new opportunity to overcome all the odds and fit every one of those angels on the head of that pin. Truthfully, no matter how many present or future projects occupy a designer's time, past failures (though long removed from public view) are never erased from her mind's eye. The same mind's eye that enables a designer to see characters, fully realized from the written word, works as an eternal reminder of every frowsy wig, overbearing print, uneven hem, and ill-fitting suit.

It would be simple to say that design failures are a matter of bad taste. I excoriate myself with that accusation every time an unsatisfactory costume or group of costumes rises up to haunt me. Frankly, I sometimes wonder if I have any consistent personal taste left — bad or good. I've gotten into the heads of so many characters that I can make a case for almost any point of view. As the internationally renowned skateboarder (who is also an artist and writer) Mark Gonzales reflects, "It's all relative to likes and dislikes." I agree. Some people detest cilantro; I love it. So there's good taste — what you have — and bad taste — what somebody else has. In group endeavors requiring the assertion of taste, it helps to work with people whose likes and dislikes are similar to yours. Assuming that everyone in a collaborative situation is doing his best, success hinges on understanding one another and being in sync. In the case of directors and designers, it is desirable to be in aesthetic sync. Such a state of coordinated perception and response is as rare as a good marriage. As in matrimony, chemistry and communication are key. Chemistry is achieved through grace, and if you don't have it, any partnership isn't much fun. Communication is essential in any case, but much easier with great chemistry. When communication falters and design failures occur, they fall into at least three categories: failures of perception, failures of execution, and failures of coordination. All successes can be lumped under the heading of minor miracles.

I have designed only one play, a production of *As You Like It*, in which I hated every single costume. It was a version of that navy-blue-skirt- and-white-blouse story elevated to a grand scale. Intimidation is not my favorite ingredient for creative engagement, and I was unabashedly cowed by the director on this production — let's call him JT. Since rumor precedes everyone in our profession, I was aware that JT, who was British, was accustomed to working "only with the best." When I was offered the job, many well-known costume designers were named as his usual collaborators. I suppose my ego didn't allow me to question why none of them was available. Paradoxically, as much as I was intimidated by JT, I was mesmerized by him in equal measure. Our first meeting took place in a small casting room on the umpteenth floor of some Westside building in New York City, and despite the grunginess of our surroundings, JT's blue eyes made the environment almost resplendent. Not a young man, he was a force of nature — intelligent, funny, emotional. And he was the most charming name-dropper I've ever met. His stories of at least three other productions of *As You Like It*, in which he had either acted with or directed some of the legendary performers of our time, gave him credentials, as far as I was concerned, to call every shot. Rarely did I consider whether I agreed with what he said about the play or the costumes. I doubt that I ventured one strong opinion in JT's presence.

Let's begin with our concept. The costumes were to be modern, but not really. While relating to contemporary clothes, they had to reflect, simultaneously, the sense of other periods, specifically the eighteenth, nineteenth, and early twentieth centuries. Such "timelessness" was not unfamiliar to me. I had faced it before *As You Like It*, and I have grappled with it since. Though it would seem oxymoronic, timelessness seems to change with the times. In the last decade or so, "deconstruction" has entered the theatrical vocabulary, subsuming "timelessness" within its boundaries. In a deconstructed production, time-traveling cultures and historical epochs are freely juxtaposed, thereby shedding light upon one another and upon the play. A turn-of-the-millennium Shakespeare is apt to feature each group of characters costumed in a period or from a country that best evokes its attitudes. The deconstructed Elizabethan court might be dressed like the Caliphates of the Abbasid Dynasty, while rustics in the same play are fitted out to resemble the Lenapes of pre-Colonial Manhattan. In this design approach, the universality of Shakespeare is the point — or is it the cleverness of the director? But, JT's production of *As You Like It* preceded any vogue for costume deconstruction. One group of characters was not supposed to coexist with another from an entirely different time and place. Ours was more of an assimilated grab-bag approach. Everyone in our play was supposed to be from the *same* eclectic time and place, where the look was kind of old-fashioned high fashion. Importantly, since *As You Like It* is a romance, the actors were to look really sexy and "fabulous." All of this, as it turned out, was to take place on a set painted bright green.

The process seemed endless. I did rough sketches. I did collages. I painted renderings. All went over very well. JT gave me explicit descriptions of what each item of clothing should look like down to the shape of a bodice and the pleat of a skirt. He picked out a fashion layout from *Vogue,* and we had to find those exact Norma Kamali suits! JT insisted on seeing just about every actor in costume after each fitting. We showed him every shoe, every hat, every scarf. When he didn't like something, I ran out searching the Northeast for whatever he thought might be better. My entire objective was to make JT happy. He knew what he was doing, and I rarely dared to ask why. Once or twice, when I did question his suddenly violent loathing for a costume (especially when I had not really designed the costume, but arranged it to what I thought were his exact specifications), I was subjected to so much pointed and, supposedly, delightful ridicule that I tried to keep any real element of my sensibility well hidden.

What did I hate most about those costumes? It wasn't until the final preview, my last time to see the production, that the blinders of pleasing JT fell away and I allowed myself to look at the whole thing critically. To my eye, the play was an uneven kitschy mess. Some of the costumes made fun of characters, others just didn't fit. We couldn't afford real Norma Kamali suits, for example, and the imitations looked like just that. The only visual element that came off well was the set. The set designer was a titan in his own right, and though JT feuded with him, the designer was not to be intimidated. From that horrible experience, I learned that unless I had the backbone to disagree with someone, I might as well quit. If I had to operate so far outside my own instincts, I wasn't the right designer for the job.

Obviously a failure of communication, my failure on *As You Like It* was more specifically a failure of perception. First of all, I don't really think the chemistry was there. Second, I didn't question JT enough to perceive a unified set of images for the play. I took down, item by item, what Jaques was supposed to wear and what Touchstone was supposed to wear. I compiled the designs, but I didn't control them. Adding one amusing element to the next, I figured that eventually the overall design would work out, sort of like a crazy quilt. The problem was that it wasn't really my crazy quilt or JT's. Rather than bad taste, there was no taste. JT had a theoretical vision of a timeless, romantic, sexy look. Though I attempted to perceive that vision as an authentic whole, I never got past JT's personal likes and dislikes. JT had a wonderful eye. I'm not being ironic, here. I truly admired his taste. Almost every individual choice he made was defendable, even captivating. It just didn't add up to a coherent version of *As You Like It*. A more effective designer should have prevailed. Great design incorporates expectation and surprise. Each element should hit a cord of recognition as it intrigues and excites. But, as everyone knows, the whole must be greater than the sum of its parts. Each person's costume should support and focus him, and it should function within the entire group of costumes to modulate and harmonize, as do the instruments in an orchestra. To achieve this, there must be a unity of perception.

Working with a director for the first time often offers the risk of producing a failure of perception. That's why producers so often ask a director to choose her own design team. Communication improves with practice. That said, I have, on other occasions, enjoyed my first-time experiences with directors. In one case, I was even younger and less experienced. The director was very worldly, and like JT, he was British. We were working on the Epic Theatre adaptation by Piscator et al. of *War and Peace*. Since the play was necessarily set in Russia during the Napoleonic Wars, establishing the time period was not a conceptual concern. In this case, achieving a shared perception was important, because of the "abstract" style of Piscator's adaptation, which had its roots in Brechtian presentational drama. Certain narration was addressed to the audience directly. The austere set included a raked upstage portion of the floor on which a map of the Russian empire was illuminated. General Kutuzov was introduced in a spotlight on one portion of this "history stage"; schematic battles were also fought there. Intimate scenes, between the Rostov family and Prince Andreii, for example, might take place downstage in relatively naturalistic interior light. Auxiliary actors were used to portray a variety of supporting characters, serfs, servants, and soldiers. The opulence of Russian aristocratic taste was key to this design, as was the pageantry of both the French and Russian Armies. But attention to vivid historic detail had to be balanced with the austerity, the bleak, film-noir, documentary quality of Piscator's script. I recently read a review of the Tchaikovsky Opera *Pique Dame* in which the reviewer Bernard Holland wrote that, "The scenes of late Eighteenth Century St. Petersburg, both indoors and out, have a studious picture-postcard correctness. Yet they . . . are factual without being particularly true." He succinctly characterizes the biggest pitfall of period re-creation. In my costumes for *War and Peace*, I believe that I came as close as I possibly could to being true to Tolstoy's characters.

From our first meeting, the director, Norman Ayerton, stimulated my confidence and curiosity. Though we were in an academic setting, with limited professional staffing, he never condescended. His knowledge was extensive but didn't hinder his ability to appreciate and encourage fresh insight. He had high standards, and many trite or familiar solutions were unacceptable to him. My job was to depict the disparate trappings of each camp — the well-born, the serfs, and the resplendent military — while creating a unity within the twentieth-century context of the script.

In addition to an engaging flow of ideas with the director, I had timing on my side for *War and Peace*. The Costume Institute at the Metropolitan Museum of Art in New York had just opened its memorable exhibit of Russian clothing from the eighteenth through twentieth centuries. A catalogue, *In the Russian Style,* edited by Jacqueline Onassis, included many of the costumes from the exhibit photographed in the Winter Palace in St. Petersburg (then Leningrad). My experience walking through those underground rooms at the Costume Institute was literally life-changing (admittedly my enthusiasms are arcane). Nothing I had ever seen or imagined in the way of color, texture, and craft had prepared me for the impact of examining those clothes, hour after hour, piece by piece. I literally became drunk on the color red. The profuse embroidery on shawls and on the borders of gowns, jackets, and waistcoats was palatably lush. I secretly harbored an egocentric belief that I was the luckiest museum-goer at the Metropolitan. I had been given the gift of redirecting some of this magnificence to the stage of the Loeb Drama Center in Cambridge, Massachusetts. I was actually moved to tears by my good fortune! I think it is fair to say that this kind of zealous engagement is the main ingredient that propelled me through the lean years of being a young, inexperienced costume designer to the marginally fatter, but emotionally more solid years of being an older, still employable one.

Having actually seen clothes that my characters might have worn, and armed with Onassis' gorgeous book as a reference, my consciousness was steeped in the world of Tolstoy's amazing story. Needless to say, I read the entire novel; its pages were explicitly illustrated in my imagination. Ayerton listened attentively to my descriptions and poured over pictures with me, adding his own observations and refinements to my choices. When I got to the point of fabric swatching, my zeal was dampened by the fact that every affordable, modern fabric and trim fell short of those beautifully embroidered silks and wools. Hand embroidery was out of the question, and we didn't really have the technology for large-scale machine embroidery. From past experimentation with fabric printing, I decided to silk-screen simplified versions of the Russian patterns and borders onto solid fabrics. Whereas most contemporary fabrics available to me were printed or woven in an all-over pattern with silk screening, we could intermittently sprig the fabric as well as concentrate larger, linear patterns on hemlines, sleeves, and shawl edges. The clean, two-dimensionality of silk screening would give unity to the various shawls, ball gowns, and waistcoats, as well as help to create the particular aesthetic reality we were trying to achieve.

Unable to build all the soldiers' uniforms, we were forced to rent, which is a matter of luck and adaptation more than design skill. In many cases, I retrimmed the jackets, pants, or hats myself, to create a look that was as extravagant as those uniforms certainly were, while still in keeping with the controlled simplicity of the silk-screened costumes. Medals figured heavily in nineteenth-century Russian uniforms. I was fortunate to find a jewelry maker who became interested in the project and made at least twenty-five or thirty gorgeous fakes, which, again, had a carefully composed artificiality that worked with the selective reality of the other costumes.

Several projects in my past stand out as being huge steps up in the quality of my work; *War and Peace* was one of them. There are times when education, experience, and present opportunity unite favorably to make one far more competent than she has ever been. My sketches for *War and Peace* were so superior to any I had previously done that I questioned whether they came from my own hand, even as I was drawing them. The final costumes were more sophisticated in cut and fit than any I had produced, and the fabric printing was startlingly effective. Most important, the costumes suited the tone of the play. In my early career, they stand out as designs successfully perceived and executed.

Back to the question of bad taste. I've implied I don't really believe in bad taste, and I hate to acknowledge my own bad taste, even though I have been in on some catastrophes that encourage me to be very hard on myself. To be kind, I will call bad taste bad execution, and like bad taste, bad execution is relative. What one designer may pull off, another cannot. I have a friend and colleague who makes brilliant drag costumes. They really are so witty, unexpected, and elegant that I respond to them with abject jealousy. Motivated by such envy, I have attempted to prove myself sufficiently outrageous and theatrical, thereby executing some really hideous mistakes.

One set of costumes still makes me cringe as it parades across my memory. In this case, developing a rapport with the director was not an issue, because he is one of my oldest and best-respected friends. My failure was purely a result of my own bad handling of a challenging opportunity. Though set in the eighteenth century, the play was a new script, definitely the product of a modern consciousness with modern dialogue. The plot involved historical people and events, but freely mixed them with fictional characters and situations. Mozart and Ben Franklin, for example, came and went in evocative cameo appearances. Parts of the play were supposed to be "really happening," while other sequences were hallucinations in the mind of the female protagonist. So, my object was to create costumes that would measure up to the audacious tone of this piece.

As always, circumstances dictated some of my design decisions. I was costuming the play concurrently with two others in a festival of new works. The costume shop was building six plays during a time period that would comfortably accommodate two at most. While the budget was adequate for a new play, no modest budget can suffice for an eighteenth-century play, particularly one in which most of the characters are well-born. With these constraints, I was casting about for a design approach when my eye fell, as has many desperate designers' eyes before it, on a layout in *Vogue* magazine. Will I never learn?! Here was an intriguing group of neo-eighteenth-century decadents. They wore period corsets made of gorgeously colored silk. The skirts were huge and full, like those of the

Rococo period, but made of layered tulle, so they seemed light and almost ethereal. The models' faces were pale and highly powdered, as was the style two hundred and fifty years ago, yet their eyes, ringed with dark colors, were incongruously now. They wore spectacular costume jewelry made of large, fake gems. Because the play was about art and artifice and was a mixture of modern sensibility with eighteenth-century situations, this fashion fantasy seemed to reflect a comparable amalgam of elements. Yes, it was a rip-off, but I would have to design additional male costumes and servants' costumes, so I termed the *Vogue* layout a "springboard."

My driving concern was to avoid being boring. Having previously seen and designed many eighteenth-century productions, I didn't want to repeat my own work or that of others. So many wonderful resources for the period are available. Take a look at the paintings of Watteau, Fragonard, Pietro Longi, or Gainsborough, to name a few. Many fine examples of clothing from the Georgian and Rococo eras exist in museums and are frequently exhibited. Period cutting patterns, made from surviving garments, are readily available in books. Aristocratic clothing of the eighteenth century is inherently theatrical and fabulously decorative. Trying to theatricalize clothing that is theatrical to begin with is a dangerous business, at least if a designer wishes to avoid the shoals of bad taste. Usually the best bet is to pick from available research and emulate what was really worn. Most audiences don't know the research and find plain ol' period recreation surprising enough. But I wanted to be more clever and unique.

Because my director trusted me, I was able to convince him that my *Vogue*-inspired design approach was going to work. He was well aware that we did not have the resources of the Metropolitan Opera available to us, so our ability to manufacture opulent finery was limited. In truth, he didn't want the clothes to look like refugees from a production of *Marriage of Figaro* or even *Don Juan*, since this piece had a darker mood. Our play had a feeling of absurdity to it, even a kind of theatrical sampling, so we agreed that some less familiar conventions for conjuring the period costumes were in order. To compound my error, I never gave the director fully rendered sketches. Time was short, so I stopped at the rough-sketch stage. Loose, out-of-proportion pencil drawings with a profusion of swatches attached are often more engaging to directors than fully painted designs. Their incompleteness allows for the hope that the final costumes will be even more wonderful. More specifically, they allow me to close a lazy eye on the problems of balance and scale that may await me.

I won't go into all the gory details: the giant, horsehair wigs, the sixties costume jewelry reworked into necklaces and stomachers, the overdyed chiffons gathered into cape linings. There may have been a few costumes that looked truly fantastical, especially in the dark scenes and especially if your taste tends toward over-the-top Fellini. Did these weird costumes actually help the play? No. The strange, time-machine, carnival look didn't make the script's turnabouts and anachronisms any more acceptable, perhaps just a bit more ridiculous.

Recently, I talked with a costumer who was in the midst of redesigning clothes for the second production of a contemporary play set in Elizabethan England. Reportedly, the mistake of the original designer was to make timeless, modern versions of Elizabethan dress, attempting to enhance the pseudo–Tom Stoppard, century-splitting tenor of the play. Since the turn of the sixteenth/seventeenth centuries is another outlandish period, in and of itself, this second designer, armed with a stupendous budget, tried to make the costumes as much like Elizabethan garments as twenty-first-century humans could arrange. Blessed with an unusually accurate sense of proportion and detail, this designer was also fortunate to have a talented and experienced costume shop behind her. The clothes really did end up looking like authentic pieces from the Victoria and Albert Museum. In my skeptical, slightly competitive fashion, I didn't believe they would suit a play so not of the Elizabethan time. Wrong. They worked perfectly for the play, kind of like gorgeous straight men. The costumes supported the conceit of time travel without further overburdening the balance of believability.

So here's where execution — or taste — comes in. Assuming most audiences do, upon occasion, enjoy costumes that imaginatively symbolize real clothing either through exaggeration, simplification, or substitution, when and how should a designer choose to reinvent rather than carefully select and imitate period research? Obviously, farce or comedy is one dramatic form well suited to outrageous reinterpretation of costume history.

Oddly, one of my favorite sets of costumes was designed for an eighteenth-century commedia dell'arte play that overlapped my above-described debacle. As yet, I had not admitted to myself that I was in trouble on the "contemporary" eighteenth-century play, being at the stage in production where resources are so far committed that a new design tack is unthinkable. A cook can't second-guess the menu after she's diced and sautéed the ingredients and is setting the table for guests who are to arrive at any minute. My subterranean sense of impending failure was undoubtedly palliated by the prospect of having an upcoming rematch with the eighteenth century. I've always believed that by the time I came to the commedia production, my research had sunk in. Having really absorbed and tested the important elements of complicated eighteenth-century silhouettes, I could reinterpret them with more assurance. I also had fewer costumes to deal with and a play in which disguise and extremity went hand in hand with the plot and acting style. Usually, I start the sketching stage of my design process with some internal fanfare and certain rituals involving my pencils, my paper, and my desk. In the case of this commedia, the final designs literally poured out of my fingers one night as I was reading the script in bed. There was no *Vogue* magazine, only my own sense of the characters and the period invigorated by what I had seen of the very unusual and inspiring set design. Though their impact was more in keeping with my fascination for strong shape, interactive color, and simplicity of detail, the costumes would eventually be some of the most outrageous and theatrical I have ever designed. I believe that I managed to execute them successfully because they were born from a genuine, personal response rather than a pandering wish to be recognized as "original."

So often, failures in my profession may be attributed to a lack of coordination. As in any field, resources in the costume world are scarce, and they must be handled judiciously. I learned early on that one of two things was necessary to costume a play: time or money. When I say time, I really mean human time, which translates to labor. Admittedly, labor can be bought if enough money is available, but in the theater, more money doesn't always mean better labor. Money, of course, will make the labor feel more fairly treated, but costume talent is uniquely passion driven. Enlisting that passion and stoking its fires is part of the costume designer's trade.

Since every costume shop is run differently and is composed of a variety of talents and personalities, a designer can go very wrong if he doesn't quickly assess the lay of the land. Almost every shop has some gap — in the craft department, for example, or the wigs. Perhaps it's a problem of understaffing: One cutter has too much to handle or too few stitchers to turn out the work. I've been in several situations, even in "wealthy" theaters, where there's no car to do the shopping, or there is a car and it belongs to the unpaid design intern and it's broken. Woe be it to the designer who doesn't cut back where talent, energy, or equipment are scarce and build up where there's more to spare.

Working with a shop for the first time, like working with a director for the first time, sometimes feels like getting through an obstacle course. I had a recent experience in an unfamiliar shop where, as it turned out, the craftsperson was abundantly talented and a demon for work, while the lone cutter's relative inexperience was compounded by the fact that she was running her own bridal business on the side. Since the cutter was a forthcoming and likeable person, while the craftsperson was a shy, slightly hermitish fellow, I was well into the build period before it dawned on me that some fancy footwork would be required if the costumes were going to come out looking at all good. After the second or third muslin fitting, when I realized that the cutter's reach far exceeded her grasp, I began to suggest less demanding construction choices for collars, sleeves, and seaming. Trying not to completely alienate the cutter, I worked to drastically reduce her input. At the same time, I shifted more emphasis to the accessories, particularly the hats. The craftsperson generously came to my rescue and went out of his way to make the hats, the dyed fabrics, the gaiters, and everything else he touched that much more outstanding. This process of effectively coordinating the labor resources is possibly the most difficult part of designing costumes.

In that it lacks the psychological complexity of identifying and utilizing the costume shop workforce, coordinating money resources is more straightforward. Even so, figuring out where to spend money and where to cut corners is always a gamble. Depending on a designer's tolerance for disregarding a budget, there is a good deal of worry and second-guessing involved. Think of how seldom any house remodeling ever costs what the owner is lead to believe it will. How often does a parent spend less than planned on Christmas or Hanukkah? Costuming, similarly, is a money pit. There are those who feel that a designer shouldn't burden a director or even himself with the unaesthetic details of a budget, but I would rather deal with scarcity as I'm designing rather than be forced to cut back after I've already promised too much.

I have come to recognize myself as a designer who works better with a limited budget than with a huge one. What can I do? I'm a product of my times. One of the first plays I helped to produce in college celebrated the life of Che Guevara! Several of the performances had to be cancelled, during Vietnam-era student demonstrations, when Cambridge police lobbed tear gas into the lobby of MIT's Kresge auditorium. My interest in theater grew from its ability to convey content and emotion simultaneously. How things looked was important insomuch as content and emotion were effectively put across. Costly display, for its own sake, must hit some guilty, puritanical, revolutionary-manqué part of me.

As a result of my Scrooge-like tendencies, my designs have become more and more cut-, color-, and character-based. I am not the designer to choose when lavish trims and ornate brocades are in order. Yes, I love gorgeous fabrics, but I can only spend so much on them before I begin to feel that I'm in the wrong theater, trying to please appetites that don't really interest me. I'm not saying that being overly pragmatic is always a good thing. As one set designer used to remind me, our greatest strength is often our greatest weakness. I have, on occasion, failed to do my job effectively by being cheap. I recently had an unbelievably generous budget to remount a previously successful farce for a large regional theater. As the process unfolded, I was told by many who had seen the play in its original incarnation that it had been a low-budget hodgepodge, pulled together brilliantly by close collaboration between the director, cast, and design team. Fearing that I would kill the production by making it too high-end, I scrounged around unnecessarily to come up with a light-hearted, unpretentious look. Instead, since this was a large main-stage production, not the little studio piece from which the play began, my work came off looking cheesy. No one, except perhaps the costume shop manager, was much impressed that the costume designer had come in under budget. This production was slated to be a big Christmas audience-pleaser, and people expected to be dazzled. Failing to dazzle has caused me some remorse. Parsimony does have its costs!

If given a choice of resources, I would always opt for skilled labor over extravagant materials. This can be pushed only so far, since even the best cutter in the world can't make really bad material look good. A certain grade of wool is requisite for tailoring; it's the only fabric that can be steamed and shaped effectively. Likewise, polyester satin will not have the same depth and luminosity onstage as will silk. Plastic is plastic and evermore shall be so. But, given this silk purse/pig's ear baseline, I'll always choose drape over rhinestones or fit over French trim. The first time I designed a small production with a really generous budget, I funneled two-thirds of my resources into hiring an Italian tailor from out of town to build the men's 1949 suits. Inevitably, there was compromise, and luckily my director agreed to it. Because the play, *The Three Cuckolds,* was a farce, we got away with having basically one costume for each male character, and we put everything into that one outfit. The resulting costumes were some of my favorite ever, not so much my doing as the tailor's. Oh to have every male garment custom-made! Resources and skills in nonprofit theater seldom allow for it. So, the "less is more" school of costume design is highly dependent on skilled draping and tailoring. Even if cut from worthy fabric, a simple, elegant garment will look no better than a glorified flour sack if it is not patterned with an artistic hand and sewn with an adept one.

How much power does a costume designer actually wield over her labor and monetary resources? The answer smacks of popular self-help-style Buddhism. You can't really control outside circumstances, or the actions of others, you can only control how you react to those circumstances and actions. A costume designer doesn't so much control the resources as she rides them, like a surfer on a breaking wave. Part luck, part agility, and part style, it's the costume designer's job to adapt to circumstances and turn them to her best advantage.

Giving a name and ascribing a cause to any failure or success implies a false sense of certainty. Undoubtedly, new, unimagined follies await anyone working in a creative field. An empty stage, with its giant, implied question mark looming in the air, is endlessly tantalizing. A working stage, filled with sets, lights, and actors in costume, sometimes falls short of the ideal. But for those who have witnessed a really great performance, who have lost track of themselves in the process of connecting with an engrossing stage reality, the theater holds perpetual promise. The question mark always offers the possibility of success. Filling a stage with costumes, on certain miraculous occasions, may contribute to an experience of beauty and insight.

Afterword

A number of years after I had finished graduate school and survived long enough as a costume designer for a fellow classmate to assume that I could take a professional insult, I was told that a third member of my class at Carnegie-Mellon had accused me of talking my way into and through the first year of our MFA program. The costumes that I described were one thing, and what I could actually draw were another. Of course, any really effective insult contains a measure of truth, and this one was no exception. I have always been a talker, and in the world of technical theater, to which costume design is inextricably linked, the motto is usually, "Put up or shut up!"

But if talking is a way of sorting through ideas, I would like to make a final case for it. In writing these essays, one point keeps emerging in my costume design worldview. The clothes eventually seen onstage are really just the tip of the iceberg. Beneath their glittering surface exists a tremendous bulk of planning and labor. To the question: What is more important about a good costume, the way it looks or what it says? I must answer emphatically: Both! Obviously, a costume can't talk — no matter how loquacious the designer. It's something to be seen and not heard, no denying that. It expresses itself through shape, texture, color, decoration (or lack thereof), fit, and movement. A costume designer must become adept at manipulating these visual elements. But the costume designer who masters the arts of coloring, draping, and trimming will arguably come up short if her visual purpose is purely superficial with no deeper examination of character, theme, and sociology.

In reviewing a 2003 biography of the famous Hollywood costume designer Edith Head, critic Adam Langer makes the inscrutable statement, "Though perhaps not the greatest costume designer in cinema history, Edith Head was the most honored." So who wins out as the "greatest costume designer" in cinema history, and on what basis? Edith Head worked for six decades designing some of the most celebrated films ever made. It would be hard to choose Hollywood's "greatest director." Among them Alfred Hitchcock, Billy Wilder, Cecil B. DeMille, William Wyler, John Ford, George Cukor, Frank Capra, and Sidney Pollock, to name a few, worked with Edith Head not once but many, many times. After the Academy of Motion Picture Arts and Sciences began to recognize costume design in 1948, Head received thirty-five nominations and eight Oscars. Lacking some of the glamour and panache attached to her more couture-oriented contemporaries such as Erte, Adrian, or her mentors Howard Greer and Travis Banton, Head, according to her 1983 biographer Paddy Calistro, gained her reputation for being able to costume stars with "problem bodies" (such as Clara Bow and Mae West), for keeping to her budgets, and for designing costumes that suited the characters and scripts. (When Head was hired by Howard Greer, by the way, she'd never done a costume sketch and later admitted to faking her portfolio with sketches made by her fellow classmates at art school. She talked her way into Paramount Studios and learned figure drawing on the job.) The actress Bette Davis, whose costumes for *All About Eve* won Head her first Academy Award, wrote of her, "While other designers were busy starring their clothes in a film, Edith was making clothes to suit a character; for her, the character always came first. . . . She always took time to read the script and understand the character. She managed to make you look as good (or as bad!) as the script allowed. If the wardrobe was to be chic, it was chic. But if the director wanted a boozy old lady like Apple Annie to be wrapped in rags in *Pocketful of Miracles*, she dressed you perfectly in character." A costume designer could not wish for a better tribute.

Though designers, like actors and painters, tend to be pigeonholed in terms of "type" and "style," the greatest ones are equally adept at script analysis as they are at decoration. Did Pat Zipprodt's degree in sociology help her create Mrs. Robinson's predatorily sexy and sophisticated costumes in Mike Nichol's movie *The Graduate*? I'd say so. Her costumes for the Broadway musical *Pippin* were equally memorable for their glorious colors, exuberant humor, and profuse textures. She, like Edith Head, had it all and could let it out or hold it back depending on what the work and the characters called for.

Every costume designer must entwine his consciousness around and within the work at hand. To do so is for some a rational process, for others an intuitive one. Whether a discursive conversation or a silent series of doodles gets you started, you're there to serve the play, the characters, and the actors. No designer has all the skills necessary at the very beginning. Working in the theater is a process of sharing and growth. Be open, adaptive, and supportive. Bring your mouth, your ears, your eyes, your hands, your sensibility, and your education, and lend them to the glory of the work!

acknowledgments

Thank you to Marisa Smith for encouraging me to write this book and for her creativity, enthusiasm, and humor along the way. Also thanks to Jon Jory for his inspiration, judicious criticism, and forward motion. Thanks to Evelyn Chen for her editorial comments. To all the costume shops and to the many stage designers with whom I've worked, it's been a tremendous pleasure learning from you.